What Others Are Saying About AMERICAN SPIN

"Spin is an old word—drawing "fiber" out and making it into a thread—that Patricia takes to a new clarity in her *American Spin.* What we learn is that spin could almost be thought of as slant. There is a story that many people know in many varying degrees of interpretation—which one is true? What is the right way of looking at it? Which…angle? Which one, and in what way, should it be "spun"?

Importantly, any learnings on spin strategy would be how to apply that thinking to yourself, your own truths in your work, your life, your dreams — and what spin could support growth and evolution? Vaccarino's *American Spin* supports that exploration. Find the right one. For you.

In a manner, as each of us studies and learns from *American Spin*, it will be: "which answer is the right spin for the stories that I am telling?" Vaccarino's journey is rich with interpretations, history lessons and learnings for each of us to know more about how the spin cycle works and how each of us could apply it to our advantage. Truth be told. But which truth? – **Tim Girvin, Principal, Girvin, Inc., Seattle, San Francisco, New York City and Tokyo**

"In *American Spin*, Patricia Vaccarino deftly separates hype and BS from true and valuable spin in the era of ubiquitous connectivity. This insightful and informative book offers real-world guidance, right on target for today's digital environment. Branding and P.R. have evolved and *American Spin* guides the reader through adoption of the necessary means and tactics to successfully get the message out in a world overabundant with avenues of communication." – **Dean Landsman, Principal, Landsman Communications Group, New York City**

"*American Spin* is very readable, smoothly juxtapositioning historic and contemporary examples of individuals, companies and techniques for building brands, conveying messages and influencing audiences to generate awareness, manage reputation and achieve goals. Its blend of "how to" with philosophy will make it a good read for people from many walks of life who I know will get a lot out of the book." – **Linda Ayares, P.R. Executive, New York City**

"Patricia not only gives the why of promoting your company and you but the how, when, where and how.....it is a blueprint to promotional success." – **Don Mazzella, Editor, Small Business Digest; Author of *An American Family Sampler*, Ridgefield, NJ**

"Before reading Patricia's book I thought I knew a thing or two about spin. Was I ever wrong! *American Spin* is a fascinating read I think everyone would benefit from, especially entrepreneurs and marketers!" – **Joe Boldan, BoldanHayes LLC; Instructor on Workplace Politics at the University of Washington; Co-founder of ExOfficio, Adventure Travel Apparel, www.boldanhayes.com, Seattle**

"One of the occupational hazards of being a reporter is a never taking anything at face value, always tugging on the hem of the curtain, pulling it back to reveal who is really spinning the cranks. In *American Spin*, Patricia Vaccarino has done that for us, showing not just the levers that are being pulled but the controls they have on what we hear and believe." – **Manny Frishberg, Journalist, Seattle, Washington**

"In *American Spin*, Vaccarino explains why the number of news sources and the speed of transmission in this age of new media calls for a thorough knowledge of how we influence others and how we are influenced in our everyday lives." – **Mimi Schroeder APR, Max Communications, Atlanta, Georgia, www.maxbookpr.com**

"In *American Spin*, Patricia Vaccarino refutes the definition of spin as being deceptive or manipulative, and takes us back to its historical origins, citing the masters of good spin. The overarching message that Vaccarino conveys in this book is that good spin must always be based on the truth. (This is particularly true in the legal profession where strict ethical rules govern advertising.) In a world inundated by social media and what Vaccarino calls the Content Bubble, she instructs on the right way to stand out of the clutter, entertaining us along the way with anecdotes and stories of spin gone wrong.

(A must read to understand the difference between good and bad spin in general, and for professionals to learn to successfully manage their reputation. The book's primary tenet is 'Do good work.' Vaccarino's book is an outstanding example of this.)" – **Donna Ross, Esq., Donna Ross Dispute Resolutions, New York City and Melbourne, Australia**

"Everybody needs a promoter and can benefit from a game plan, a strategy and counsel from an experienced P.R. professional. In *American Spin*, Patricia shows the complexity of spin and why it's difficult to promote yourself." – **Lori Randall, Principal, Randall PR, Seattle**

"If you think you're going to win the content game without this book, think again. If you think you can rest on your laurels, think again, for there are those without any who will beat you to the punch. To truly live in America and in the world, Vaccarino asserts spin should be a crucial element of our education. This book is a great start." – **Robbin Block, Blockbeta Marketing, Seattle**

"A cross between Sir Edward Bernays *Propaganda* and Machiavelli's *The Prince*, Patricia Vaccarino's *American Spin* is not your ordinary how-to P.R. book. Chapter headings such as "You can get away with murder" and "Evil comes in many shades of gray" will give individuals and organizations a refreshing look at the spin that dominates our culture and how we can use spin to our own advantage." – **Joseph M. Puggelli, Educator, Seattle**

American Spin

by Patricia Vaccarino

How spinmeisters tell you what to think about people, products, issues and companies

Printed in the United States of America

First Edition: May 2015

Xanthus Communications
2212 Queen Anne Avenue North PO #615
Seattle, WA 98109

American Spin is a PR for People® book

Dedicated to

My husband Joseph M. Puggelli

and to my three children:

David, Katie, and Sarah

Contents

Acknowledgements

American Spin would not be complete unless I mention gratitude to my husband, Joe Puggelli, for being my life partner, collaborator, lover, intellectual companion and inspiration.

I thank my clients for giving me the opportunity to get the deserved recognition for who they are and what they do.

I also thank the many journalists that I have had the privilege to work with through the years.

Special thanks to Hall Stuart-Lovell and Josue Mora for their superb work on the design and layout for *American Spin*.

Preface

American Spin explores what lies beneath news gathering, news reporting, and brings to the forefront the economic realities that shape the news you hear, see, or read every day. Throughout my career in P.R., I've pitched stories to many publications, and I've frequently succeeded getting my spin placed in all facets of the media: internet, broadcast (radio and TV), cable, and print, both in magazine and daily news format. As a seasoned P.R. professional, it is my mission to educate people about how Spin is made. *American Spin* is meant to empower people so they can effectively communicate their own stories to the world.

I wrote *American Spin* in Seattle, Washington, home to the Space Needle, the Seahawks, the Mariners, and the gray squall of incessant rain. Seattle is located in the far northwest corner of the country and is surrounded by water: Lake Union, Lake Washington, and the Puget Sound. To the south Mount Rainier juts up like an enormous snow-cone. The city is bordered by two mountain ranges, the Cascades in the east and the Olympics to the west. Both ranges are topped with snow year round. Seattle is proud of its mountains, water, and clotted gray bank of clouds. The climate is moderate, with the average annual temperature ranging between forty and sixty-five degrees Fahrenheit.

Old Seattle was composed of several generations of original settlers and heavily populated by people of Irish, Anglo, Scandinavian, and Asian descent. The rise of major companies such as Microsoft, Amazon, and Starbucks brought an influx of talent into the area from all over the United States, as well as from Europe and Asia. In the last twenty years, Seattle has grown up and has developed maturity and a powerful place in the world. *New Seattle* is composed of people who are highly educated, prosperous, and said to be part of the creative class that is emerging in those American cities that have strong technology companies along with major research universities.

The rise of Seattle's creative class, coupled with a strong investor community, creates an ideal environment for talent, innovation, and new companies to flourish.

And yet, despite the physical beauty of Seattle, it rains frequently and you can hardly see the mountains. The traffic in Seattle is so bad during rush hour that it takes nearly an hour to get from one part of the city to another. Most housing prices are skyrocketing; apartments and homes are priced so high that most people can't afford to live here unless they're technology workers. Seattle is an extremely tribal culture and people generally only become friends with those whom they know through school, work, or church. Everyone else tends to get shut out. The Seattle Freeze, or the way Seattleites ignore newcomers, outsiders, and out-of-towners, is legendary and no one can explain the phenomenon. Seattleites have a reputation for being nice, polite, and often helpful. But try inviting *new Seattle friends* to dinner or a networking event. They will say *Maybe*, which is a polite way of saying no.

What I have stated about Seattle is indisputably true, but which version is the real truth? Is Seattle a dynamic community that allows startups to flourish, or is it an overpriced and overcrowded city that snubs its newcomers? Both views of Seattle are true and they are also both a form of *gentle* spin. Neither perspective is all good or all bad. The distinguishing characteristics are quite subtle and either story can be told about Seattle when you want to achieve a certain outcome. My guess is if you're an HR recruiter working for Amazon you will want to spin the selling of Seattle to a new hire in the most positive light possible. If you want to dissuade people from moving to Seattle, another version of the city's profile can easily be told.

No matter which way you present Seattle to friend or foe, to job-seekers or companies seeking relocation, to the press or to the Olympic Games committee, the facts you weave together to tell the *Seattle* story must be undeniably true in order to create a specific impression. *Good spin must always resonate as the truth.*

Patricia Vaccarino

1

Good Spin is a Way of Packaging the Truth

Why should you care about spin? In today's unceasing crush of information, everyone must conduct effective Public Relations (P.R.) to break through the clutter to get heard or to get seen. Building a brand, getting a job, keeping a job, building a business, making sales, increasing sales, winning political elections, getting funding for a business or for an organization, recruiting workers and top talent—all rely on crafting effective spin and getting quality placement in the media. In today's world, we have too little time and we are inundated with too much information. People must examine how spin can be utilized to serve their own best interests. Regardless of your occupation or your audience, you need to treat the creation of your spin with the same intensity as if you were an entrepreneur who is building a business.

Everyone is obliged to conduct effective P.R. Becoming savvy about P.R. and utilizing P.R. tools has become critical due to our dependence on technology and the speed in which information is communicated. P.R. is now much more than media relations or community-building. In the new world order, P.R. has become an art form that strategically creates spin in order to get your message to your desired target audience. Here is a bold assertion: by understanding how spin works and by embracing its subtle nuances, you will achieve greater success in business and attain a higher level of critical thinking that will enhance your own life so your thinking is grounded in reality. Ultimately, good P.R. should be designed and managed to get what you want out of life.

The primary tool used in P.R. is spin. Spin is the best way to take complex information and distill it into a platform that can be quickly communicated to the audience. Although spin makes it possible to convey complex information quickly, more importantly, it also increases the likelihood that your audience will understand your information. Sometimes people think because they have jobs they might not need to utilize spin as a P.R. tool to build their brand. It could not be farther away from the truth. If we didn't utilize spin as a great communications tool, we would not be able to tell stories that are timely, compelling, and memorable. And most important of all, good spin will get an audience to take some sort of action: buy, sell, vote, give up using plastic bags, support gay marriage, or get the green light for a new corporate project. The precise call of action has no limits. Without spin we wouldn't be able to get people to take action.

Spin is the subtle layering of facts to establish an emotional connection between the storyteller and the audience. So, to some extent, it's unfair to cast spin in a negative light. Spin allows people, businesses of all sizes, non-profit organizations, and governments to influence the masses. Spin has been around since the beginning of time and it will never go away so long as there is a need to influence a majority of people. What is unusual about spin in today's world is the speed in which information is disseminated on a global scale. The other differentiating factor is that so many entities are all spouting spin at the same time, which means the spin you create must be superior. It does not matter what business you are in or if you are in business at all. Whether you are in politics, banking, finance, agriculture, manufacturing, education, technology, the arts, entertainment, or charity, you must have a messaging platform, and you must spin your story to the world.

Edward Bernays is widely considered to be the founding father of what is now commonly known as modern Public Relations. In his landmark 1928 treatise on P.R., called *Propaganda*, Bernays freely admits, "There is no word in the English language that has been so badly distorted as the word *propaganda*. The change took place mainly during the late war when the term took on a decidedly sinister complexion."

While Edward Bernays wrote *Propaganda* almost a century ago, in reality little has changed.

Everyone should have an understanding of P.R. and how spin works. Learning how to spin and how to work with the media is a life skill that is as important as learning how to read, write, and speak in one's native language. A good education in spin means people must examine how spin-in-the-news can benefit them or how it can cause them harm. School children should study P.R. as a method to develop critical thinking skills so they can make good decisions about what they hear, see, and read about in the press. Also, many great stories do not get written up or reported in the press, and throughout this book we shall examine why.

What is Spin?

Toy tops spin. Dancers spin. In Public Relations, the definition of spin is the positioning from which a story is told. Spin is essential artful storytelling. Spin is the exact way a story is told. It's the precise way facts are sliced and diced. Spin is also the sequence or layering of facts and the exact order in which the facts are presented to the intended recipient. Spin is created by propaganda, also known as *the message*. Often associated with propaganda, spin has a bad name. The real foundation for any P.R. initiative is rooted in propaganda. Keep in mind the very concept of *Propaganda* was created by the Catholic Church. The College of Propaganda at Rome, the *Sacred College of Propaganda Fide,* was founded by Pope Urban VIII in 1627 to educate missionary priests.

The Catholic Church has always been masterful in its use of propaganda, spin, and storytelling. The story about Pope Francis picking up a random hitchhiker in Vatican City traveled around the world in a nanosecond. The press was on this story like a gaggle of geese. *Can you imagine being an ordinary person standing on the road hitchhiking a ride and the Pope picks you up! Wow!* It was one more notch in the papal belt for a man who stands for humility, a strong commitment to social justice, and compassion for the poor—he's the people's pope.

Only it turns out the hitchhiker was not a random guy on the street. In a crowd of 50,000 people, Pope Francis spotted

Reverend Father Fabian Baez, a parish priest at the Our Lady of the Pillar church, which was the Pope's former Archdiocese of Buenos Aires. After the priest climbed into the *popemobile*, the Pope told him, "The picture will go around the world." Even Father Fabian Baez has his own Twitter account @paterfabian.

The best propaganda feeds facts that are indeed accurate to the masses. Yes it is true! Pope Francis is the *People's Pope!* He does live alone in a tiny, Spartan apartment. He does ride on public transportation and cooks his own meals. He does reject pomp and ornamental vestments. He did choose the papal name *Francis* to honor Saint Francis of Assisi and to demonstrate his concern for the poor. The spin or angle of this story is that the Catholic Church has a new spiritual leader who cares about the Church's followers.

The appointment of Pope Francis is the Catholic Church's strategic deployment of crisis management and damage control. The Catholic Church had to do something about its tarnished reputation for providing a culture of pedophilia and harboring pedophiles. In America, the number of church members has plummeted; schools and whole parishes have become extinct. Yet the church owns substantial holdings, especially real estate, all tax-free. With a US economy in turmoil and a trillion dollar deficit, it is only a question of time before the constitutional separation between church and state is re-examined. Think of all the revenue the Catholic Church could contribute to the American economy if only it paid taxes like everyone else. During a critical time in the church's history, replacing the dour pragmatist *Benedict XVI with Francis, the People's Pope, is a brilliant business strategy.* Pope Francis is much more than the People's Pope; he's really a turnaround CEO. Under the leadership of Pope Francis, they are doing a full-out P.R. campaign. No one does P.R. better than the Catholic Church.

Historically, spin has been with us since the beginning of time. Edward Bernays in his classic treatise, *Propaganda,* referred to Emily Ludwig who practiced P.R. during the Napoleonic era. "Emily Ludwig represents Napoleon as ever on the watch for indications of public opinion; always listening to the voice of the people, a voice which defies calculation."

There is nothing all that new about P.R. and the concept of spin. Bernays suggests that with Propaganda, what we now know as spin, "The minority has discovered a powerful help in influencing majorities. It has been found possible so to mold the mind of the masses that they will throw their newly gained strength in the desired direction. Whatever of social importance is done today, whether in politics, finance, manufacture, agriculture, charity, education, or other fields, must be done with the help of propaganda."

Romans + the Rubicon = Ancient Spin

In the ancient world, P.R. was practiced in discreet whispers and loud shout-outs among spies and influencers with the same intense engagement as mommy bloggers and live Twitter feeds. When it comes to using P.R. as a tool to build a brand, people fall into two camps: Those who use P.R. as a way to manage their reputations and those who summarily dismiss P.R. as if it's a grain of salt. Here are two opposing case studies from the ancient world: Julius Caesar and the first Emperor of Rome, Caesar Augustus.

Julius Caesar, one of the greatest military minds in history, crossed the Rubicon River in northern Italy. The Roman general could not bring his army across the Rubicon and into Italy without facing a civil war. He wasn't supposed to go there. He broke the rules. The expression "Crossing the Rubicon" is hardwired in our culture as another way of saying, *there is no turning back*. It is the equivalent of burning your bridges. According to reliable sources, as soon as he crossed the river, Caesar uttered the time worn phrase *āleaiactaest*, "the die is cast."

The resulting struggle pitted the armies of Julius Caesar against the armies of the Roman Senate. Military genius Julius Caesar won the civil war, but he never won the war of popular opinion enough to create a groundswell of support to become Emperor. He didn't have a strong P.R. arm to get the word out to win support for his triumphs, his accomplishments, and for his prowess as a leader of the ancient world.

Aside from getting the word out, a good P.R. person always has her ear to the ground to gather intelligence, to detect chatter, and to assess emerging trends for strategic positioning. And, if need be, to make clever preemptive strikes.

Some newly emerging social media gurus claim the art of listening is new, but they're just clueless. Listening well has been around since the beginning of time. Julius Caesar didn't have anyone who had his ear to the ground and who could communicate crisis and danger. Without a P.R. advisor, Julius Caesar walked into the forum alone and met his untimely death.

Unlike Julius Caesar, the young Caesar Augustus was frail and lacking the robust physicality required of Roman military leaders like Julius Caesar or Marc Antony. But young Caesar Augustus understood the power of P.R. It was his trusted P.R. Counsel, Gaius Maecenas, who guided him from being *Octavius* to becoming *Octavian* to his ultimate transformation into *Caesar Augustus*—the first Emperor of Rome.

One ancient story depicts the young Octavius jumping over barricades into a besieged city during a battle to demonstrate two prized attributes in the Roman world: strength and heroics. The sight of Octavius jumping over artfully placed barricades and appearing to be as large and as grand as Julius Caesar crossing the Rubicon was a silly stunt even for most ancient audiences. Everything had been set up in advance and staged. There was never a stray second when Octavius could have been in any real danger. The whole scene had been theatrically staged by the wily master of perception, Gaius Maecenas, who was described by an elder statesman of Rome as being "of sleepless vigilance in critical emergencies, far-seeing, and knowing how to act." Aside from guiding the young Caesar Augustus through many landmines to become Emperor, history credits Gaius Maecenas as being integral to the establishment of the new world order— the Roman Empire, which initiated the *Pax Romana*, the Roman peace that lasted for over two hundred years.

Fast forward to the post-modern world where eighty percent of what is reported in the press has been placed there by P.R. people who were paid to spin a story and pitch it to the media. In every news story, you can spot the original source of the story: a company, an individual, a non-profit organization, a cause, a school, the government; everyone has a story and it's told through the lens of a P.R. firm or a publicist. In every news story that you read, see, or hear, you must ask yourself: Who placed the story? Was it a person, a company, an organization, or an industry coalition?

Positive spin or negative spin? It's always a matter of positioning—the facts that were told and the facts that were left out. Most news stories seem as though they're balanced and tell all sides of a story, but if you examine any news story, you will see there is always a definite slant. In everything you read, everything you hear, and everything you see, ask yourself: Who is the source? What is the source trying to accomplish? Is the source looking for a *come up*? Or is the source trying to bring someone down? We are inundated with so much clutter that our attention span flickers and we scan news accepting the basic facts as the truth. Always keep in mind, the press doesn't necessarily lie, but it is never required to tell the whole truth.

What is the Difference Between Good Spin and Bad Spin?

Knowing how to create spin that achieves a desired outcome isn't as easy as it might seem. There is good spin and bad spin. Good spin is simply a good story well told that grabs your attention and gets you to feel powerful emotion. Bad spin, on the other hand, is mostly based on lying. There are three forms of bad spin. One form of bad spin is boldfaced lying, the way the U.S government positioned Saddam Hussein as a terrorist. Sooner or later bad spin will be exposed as a lie that reaps a groundswell of negative public opinion and destroys trust.

Edward Bernays noted his rationale for bad spin in *Propaganda*: "The instruments by which public opinion is organized and focused may be misused. But such organizing and focusing are necessary to orderly life." It is not unusual for governments and institutions of all sizes to lie because it is the easiest and most effective way to control the public.

Another form of bad spin is hype. Hype is when someone gets excited about something they have done and creates an excessive amount of publicity and noise that far exceeds the integrity or intrinsic value of the news post. As an example, on Facebook, one new author recently stated, "My first book is currently #15 on Amazon in the literary short stories section. Awesomeness! If I can move up 11 spots, I'll be able to bump Rudyard Kipling. Goal!" Usually the person's work cannot live up to the expectations created by the hype. Whenever you suspect the spin is full of hype, consider the source. It is unlikely a first time self-published author has the gravitas to unseat the work and legacy of Rudyard Kipling.

Bad spin thinly disguised as hype is found everywhere on social media and especially on Twitter.

Consider the following thread of hysterical tweets: "Justin Bieber's grandparents were in a car crash! Justin Bieber's grandparents' car flipped! How are Justin Bieber's grandparents? Are Justin Bieber's grandparents alive or dead? OMG!! Justin Bieber really loves his grandparents!!!"

I don't follow Justin Bieber and I really don't care about his grandparents, but I Googled the story. Then I realized what I was doing. I was getting sucked into news that was totally irrelevant to anything in my business or my life. I got hooked by the story: drama, tragedy, imminent death, and grief, an accident so horrific that the car flipped in the air and landed upside down. OMG! Justin Bieber may have lost his grandparents!

Whether it's told in 140 characters or in a book, an article, a blog, or a video, a good story will always command attention, even when it's hype.

In the last few years, people have been giving up newspapers and TV news and keeping up with late-breaking news via Twitter. Ordinary people are sharing information and telling compelling stories that may or may not be true. Twitter spouts word-of-mouth chatter like a nasty super virus. Sooner or later you are going to catch the bug. You just don't know how bad your symptoms will be and how long it will take for you to recover.

Twitter is making news more social and dramatic than it has ever been in the past. The question remains: will Twitter get you clients, increase sales, and grow your business? With Twitter, it is hard to separate who is authentic from the poseurs. A large following may look impressive, but it is increasingly common to buy followers from teams in India who grow Twitter followers the same way black hat Search Engine Optimization (SEO) tactics generated content farms and false links to boost websites' search rankings on Google. People who have large Twitter followings do not always have a real community, but may have paid to buy a mercenary herd of followers that is transported from one social media account to another.

Does Ashton Kutcher really have over ten million followers or is his magic genie a silk-turbaned Sikh team working in India for $2 an hour?

Twitter offers no accountability to assess what is genuine news vs. rumormongers, carpetbaggers, and snake oil salesmen. Twitter offers no authentication to truly know who is really tweeting behind the scenes. Twitter is more than the Wild West. It's a gold rush where no one knows what is real and what is hype.

OMG!! What happened to Justin Bieber's grandparents? They were scared and shaken-up, but they're okay!!! This sort of spin crafted to promote Justin Bieber is pure hype.

The downside to using hype as the bedrock for your spin is that you never know how long a tail you will grow or how long that tail will live. The late Roy Amara was a researcher, a scientist, and a past president of the Institute for the Future. He also worked at the Stanford Research Institute. He had a Ph.D. in Systems Engineering, and he also had an M.S. in Arts and Science, which gave him a unique perspective to see both the forest and the trees. He is known for Amara's Law: "We tend to overestimate the effect of a technology in the short run and underestimate the effect in the long run."

Technology and the speed of digital communications intensify the impact of spin and increase the length of its tail. The speed and intensity of spin is all the more reason why spin must be precise, strategically well-thought-out, and grounded in reality. Good spin should never be an outright lie. Spin doesn't simply invent the truth. When spin is based on fabrication, pure fiction, no one will believe it, at least not forever. In fact, quite the opposite will happen. Bad spin can undo your persona; it can ruin your reputation and cause irreparable harm.

As much as I have cautioned clients, colleagues, family, and friends about being prudent and exercising good judgment about what to post on social media, and especially on Facebook, I am constantly amazed by the embarrassing things people put out there for the whole world to see. Why do people go out of their way to create their own bad spin?

The motives are manifold: to get attention, love, adoration; maybe to shock. Or sometimes the reason could be sheer stupidity or boredom. A 2014 study by FindLaw.com found that 29 percent of adults aged 18-34 fear that something they've posted on social media could jeopardize their current or future job prospects; and 74 percent say they've removed something from their social media to avoid a negative backlash. There is great danger in using hype as spin.

A third form of bad spin is when the spin or angle of the story was all wrong for the audience. I once observed a keynote speaker, who was a celebrated marketing expert, using case studies featuring Prada, Gucci, and Louis Vuitton—all luxury fashion brands. The audience was composed of wealthy male techies whose idea of fashion was to wear two-socks-that-matched with their Birkenstocks. I watched the audience for reaction and saw blank expressions, squirming in squeaky chairs. They were more riveted by their mobile phones than they were by the speaker.

The marketing professional who gave the talk was so intent on extolling his own image that he lost sight of his audience and spun out. If an experienced marketer can make this mistake, so can you. Later we will devote attention to why you should always know your target audience. And how to connect with the target audience. This does not mean that you dilute the integrity of your message. It does mean that you must adjust your spin so your audience gets what you are talking about.

At the heart of good spin, you will always find the truth. And the best manipulative device is often the truth. So there isn't anything inherently wrong with spin; it is neither right nor wrong, good or bad, moral or immoral. Edward Bernays said, "It may seem an exaggeration to say that the American public gets most of its ideas in this wholesale fashion. The mechanism by which ideas are disseminated on a large scale is propaganda, in the broad sense of an organized effort to spread a particular belief or doctrine."

It is important to keep in mind that Bernays wrote about these truths in 1928 and how much more challenging it is today to disseminate ideas in the current crush of information. In the 21st century, we need spin as an artful way to package the truth so we can break through the clutter. If the truth is not packaged well, and spun well, it doesn't stand a chance of breaking through the clutter.

Good Spin Gone Viral: The "Kaling" of America

When truth is packaged well it can take over the world. Take kale. A network of giant food retailers, commercial farmers, health food chains, wholesale food vendors, and other ancillary businesses have created a phenomenon that can be described as the *Kaling of America*. Essentially, we're talking about P.R. for vegetables. There isn't a vegetable out there that cares whether it's popular enough to be eaten. Lately there has been an explosion in popularity for this green leafy vegetable, kale. This is an especially important observation because two years ago the consumption of kale was *de minimus*, and now there are mountains of kale everywhere. Kale has become the darling of foodies and celebrity chefs, who are trading recipes across all media points. Some studies indicate kale is now on 400 percent more restaurant menus than it was before the green explosion. At Trader Joe's, plastic bags of kale, organic and regular (I can't tell them apart), vastly outnumber bags of pre-washed romaine lettuce, spinach, and arugula, and the lowliest green thing of all—broccoli.

One night, I was waiting between meetings and staked a spot at a new healthy fast food eatery called *Evolution*, where I had a bowl of veggie quinoa soup that was loaded with guess what?? Kale! Soon I found myself in the middle of a marketing event where a detox outreach team showed up to promote colonic cleansing and handed out little plastic cups of kale juice. Did you know that 1 cup of kale contains sustenance far greater than your daily requirements: 190 percent of Vitamin A, 90 percent of Vitamin C, mega doses of B6, Manganese, Calcium, Copper, and Potassium. Studies have shown that kale protects your eyes from the sun and prevents cataracts. The enzymes in kale trigger cancer fighting chemicals that eliminate unhealthy cells throughout your entire body, and when animals with tumors are given a diet of kale, their tumors shrink.

Oh My! Those clever kale P.R. people! Kale is much more than a vegetable; it's the holy grail of the 21st century, the fountain of youth, and the chief arbiter of world peace. These are just some of the benefits!

When even a vegetable is spinning stories to the public, someone has paid a mighty price for an enormous budget dedicated to a full-scale marketing and P.R. outreach.

Kale is easy to grow, relatively bug and disease resistant, produces a high crop yield, and even does well in freezing weather. In fact, a sudden frost actually gives kale a sweeter taste. Why not create a market demand for kale? The fact that the popular leafy vegetable took over the western world is an example of great spin because it's true! Kale is actually good for you and a clarion call to healthy eating! Behemoth chain grocery stores are getting a higher Return On Investment (ROI) for selling kale than for selling other greens. Kale is not alone in its surging popularity. Remember the past campaigns for raisins, prunes, and blueberries? If even vegetables need P.R., then so do you. People have to create awareness for how well their services and expertise compare to what everyone else is offering. All of which begs the question: What P.R. strategy do you have in place for yourself?

2

The Problem with the Media

Entrepreneurs who use P.R. to promote themselves or their business will invariably run into a major problem. A rumor about a celebrity or a politician can get posted on a blog or Twitter and get picked up as news story within minutes. And yet, if you are an entrepreneur who is diligently promoting what you consider a good story to the press, it can easily be rejected. With so many new media outlets emerging every day, it should be easy to get placed in the press. In fact quite the opposite is true. It is more challenging than ever for entrepreneurs to get solid media placement and to gain traction for their businesses.

Even P.R. professionals deal with the same problem—their spin can be ignored when it isn't newsworthy enough to command media attention and break through the clutter.

The man I called the *Big Kahuna* grew up as a surfer boy in southern California. In 2001, I was the head of P.R. at a technology company where the Big Kahuna was second-in-command. Beefy, with thinning hair, the Big Kahuna was in his mid-fifties, wore suspenders and occasionally smoked cigars. I once met the Kahuna's trophy wife during our one and only lavish company holiday party. A big blonde with platinum hair down to her waist, she wore a slinky, black jumpsuit, and tottered on six-inch *Christian Louboutin* heels.

The Big Kahuna wanted to send a press release announcing the arrival of *his company*. It is what we call a stake-in-the-ground press release. The problem? It wasn't news. The company employed nearly 100 people, wasn't exclusively his and had been around for two years before the Big Kahuna came on board. Everyone in technology, including the press, already knew the company existed. Sending out a press release announcing the existence of a company—one that had been around for two years with unproven technology and no revenue—wasn't a feature news story. I told the Kahuna a press release wouldn't generate much press pickup. He summarily dismissed my counsel and said, "Our technology is so groundbreaking that this press release is going to rock the world!"

The day the press release went out over the wire, the largest conference room in the company was set up as a war room. Extra chairs, tables, and computers were jammed into the room. Three additional phones were wired in. The Kahuna hauled in a white board, an overhead projector, and a wide screen so we could monitor each media placement as if it was military advancement into an enemy camp. Orders were placed for takeout Chinese to be delivered. The room was loaded with flats of water, Diet Pepsi, and snacks. The entire marketing team was summoned to sit and hold vigil in this room that had come to resemble a bomb shelter. The Kahuna toyed with a big fat cigar and checked his watch. The press release crossed the wire at 8 a.m. Eyes fastened on the phones where the tiny red jewel lights did not flash. In fact, nothing happened.

Finally, one phone line buzzed and everyone jumped. But it wasn't the press. It was the receptionist calling to let us know our takeout food had arrived. Miraculously, by the next day, the press release was picked up in seven media outlets—as business news, a few column-inch mentions. No feature coverage.

P.R. with the Big Kahuna took place 12 years before the rise of social media and the decline and fall of the *legacy* (traditional) press. Back in the day, when you sent a press release over the wire, you would get an amazing surge of traffic to your website—thousands of hits—that is if you had a good spin to your story. Nowadays, even a press release that is telling a good story will only get a tiny spike in traffic. The huge bombardment of information has made it so that the telling of any story must be sustained for months, if not years, to penetrate the clutter.

Unfortunately for the Big Kahuna, his company had run out of time. The month after our expensive holiday party, I learned the company had burned through millions of dollars and was unable to get bridge financing. The entire staff of nearly 100 was laid off, including me and the Big Kahuna. He moved back to southern California where he took a job selling hedge funds.

The Big Kahuna had the right idea about setting up a war room, but he suffered two major weaknesses. First, he didn't have a story. The press already knew about the company, but it had unproven technology and it was quickly running out money. Second, the Big Kahuna suffered from the hubris of believing the company would be an overnight success. Creating awareness for a person, product, or company isn't done in one day.

Every P.R. campaign needs to be waged with the strategic precision of war for months and even years. The victory of each ensuing battle is really just preparation for the next campaign, i.e., the next battle. Entrepreneurs who use P.R. understand that it will take many decisive victories to win a war. Entrepreneurs who use P.R. must be armed with the best practices in order to wage effective media relations campaigns to win the favor of the press. In order to be effectively armed, let's take a look at the state of media as an industry. Here is some business intelligence from the ground.

Content Bubble

As a P.R. professional who labors to break through the clutter to reach the right target audiences, I am in close contact with the looming specter called the *Content Bubble*. The average American spends at least eight and a half hours a day in front of a screen, Nicholas Carr notes in his book *The Shallows*.[1] The number of hours American adults spend online doubled between 2005 and 2009, and the number of hours spent in front of a TV screen is steadily increasing. Seventy-two hours of video are uploaded to YouTube every minute. Five hundred years of YouTube video are watched every day on Facebook, and over 700 YouTube videos are shared on Twitter each minute. Please note that these numbers are only valid for a moment and are perpetually on the rise.

And yet the latest research from Pew Internet shows 84 percent of Facebook news feed stories aren't viewed, 71 percent of tweets get ignored, and 88 percent of emails go unopened. As a result of the Content Bubble, the transmission of information, even if it is important and merits our attention, can be ignored. Email used to be the most effective way to reach an audience, and it no longer holds true today. Email is no longer the fastest, smartest, or best way to reach an audience. Email has slowed down, and while it has not yet reached the point of extinction, it has definitely become part of the Content Bubble.

Everyone is overwhelmed by the Content Bubble. People cannot keep up. The Content Bubble has yet to produce a sustainable business model. We need new ways to filter content that only allows the most timely, relevant, and compelling information to rise to the top. Meanwhile, we all have to deal with a bottleneck clogged with a backlog of unviewed email, books, articles, posts, photos, and movies.

There is also a power struggle taking place among media heavyweights who are jockeying to control the media. Media "moguls" like Rupert Murdoch, Mort Zuckerman, the Dolan family, and Jeff Bezos are intent on dominating media the same way the big industrialists dominated the railroads at the beginning of the last century. Who will live and who will die? Only time will tell. Top-tier media outlets like NBC's *The Today Show* and *The New York Times* are feeling the stranglehold and keep struggling for new ways to reinvent themselves to increase eyeballs and advertising revenue. There is so much competition no one can get market share. The Press is vying for market share by posting the most sensational, attention-grabbing headlines—often Yellow Journalism.[2] If you are not sure what yellow journalism is, pop online to cnn.com and scan the first five stories, and you will see headlines that are sensational, slightly hysterical, and a distorted presentation of the facts. Many media outlets are just looking at the numbers—revenue and traffic—and not necessarily at the quality of journalism.

The goal of all media outlets is to go viral at all costs. Legacy media (traditional press) is obsessed with social media because emphasis is placed on the media's ability to increase its social reach. Tremendous pressure is placed on editors, reporters, producers, freelance writers, and journalists-of-all-stripes to devote as much time as possible to amplify their news coverage on social media, especially on Twitter.

In the post-modern age, the increasing reliance on social media has caused legacy media to become highly fragmented. Created by digitization and accelerated by the recession, the meltdown of the media as an industry has created fragmented audiences and broken business models. Many forms of media are highly fragmented because they only target niche or special audiences. Media fragmentation is increasing and creating more media than there has ever been in the past. And it is making it very difficult for any of us to break through the ice to be seen and heard above the din.

Ice is a good metaphor for clutter. It is the media that is creating a lot of the clutter. Ice is also a good metaphor for our life and times—a great way to describe a credit freeze, a housing freeze and the frozen job markets. Ice causes all kinds of systems to seize up.

For you to build your brand in the current climate, your greatest battle is waging war against clutter which is as deep and as powerful as an iceberg. Breaking through the clutter requires moving like an icebreaker through a field of ice. An icebreaker moving against a field of ice is relentless and powerful. The icebreaker has a strong engine, and by steadily boring away over time, it will break through the ice. Well-crafted spin cuts through the clutter of information the way an icebreaker cuts through a freezing ocean full of icebergs. Entrepreneurs can harness the media as a tool to break through the clutter. Entrepreneurs have a great opportunity to gain traction and to take market share at a faster rate than they have in the past. In order to achieve success in the new media world, entrepreneurs will need to embrace P.R. tools and the best practices of *American Spin* to cut the path through the labyrinth of clutter and reach the right audiences.

When dealing with the media, there is one other factor to explore, and that is the issue of trust. To further complicate the problem of dealing with a chaotic and fragmented media, in the maelstrom of clutter, the world is sending us extreme mixed messages about what is right and what is wrong. Perhaps we lack the wisdom to know what is right or wrong, and fail to deal properly with the moral conundrum of our world in the 21st century. It's no wonder we have a crisis of confidence that has beset our culture. There has been some conjecture that the crisis of confidence is at the highest ever since the Great Depression in 1929. Edward Bernays wrote *Propaganda* close to the same year as the onset of the Great Depression. In a similar vein, *American Spin* is grappling with a crisis of confidence in the age of new media, where we have many more media outlets than have ever existed in the past.

We have witnessed a meltdown of legacy media and a dramatic rise of social media that has created a multitude of small fragmented audiences. There is no single channel of communication to reach the entire population, such as radio during World War II, or the early days of television in the 1950s and 60s, when three channels dominated the market.

On all fronts in every sector, there are multitudes of media voices all shouting at the same time. And so the question must be asked: In whom do you trust?

On the surface there appear to be many choices for the typical consumer to get his or her news. In reality there is only the *illusion of choice*. An eye-opening report in *Business Insider*[3] claims that only six corporations control 90 percent of all media outlets. The big six media giants—Comcast, News Corp., Disney, Viacom, Time Warner, and CBS—control 90 percent of what we read, see, or hear in the news. The big six media conglomerates have consolidated from the 50 companies that existed in 1983. And back in 1928 when Edward Bernays wrote his classic P.R. treatise, *The American Newspaper Annual and Directory* listed 22,128* periodical publications in America; many were small businesses, owned by individuals.

*Number sourced from Edward Bernays' classic treatise on Propaganda

While news is transmitted rapidly, it is disseminated though what appear to be many discordant and competing outlets. One person might get his news from TV and another from Twitter or the radio or *The New York Times* or a regional daily newspaper. While we are all receiving information that is sanctioned by a relatively small number of media executives who control the flow of information, there is no one news source that we respect and trust. In the current climate of media disruption, there is no centralized news source that offers high quality original news content and as well as the aggregation of content from many other news outlets to create a *single trusted news authority*.

On the Frontlines of Authentic Journalism

In the late 19th century in Paris, the great writer Émile Zola set the standard for what we have come to define as authentic investigative journalism. Through his landmark article "*J'accuse,*" Zola accused high levels of the French Army and the French government of having wrongfully convicted Captain Alfred Dreyfus on trumped-up charges of obstruction of justice. As a result of those charges, Dreyfus had been sentenced to life imprisonment. Émile Zola's feature article delving into the Dreyfus Affair was published on the front page of the Paris daily, *L'Aurore,* which back then was the equivalent of today's *New York Times.* Sparking a heated political and social controversy, the Dreyfus Affair threatened to unravel the very foundation of the French government in a nation that was already deeply divided between an out-of-control French army, an anti-Semitic and corrupt Catholic church, and the French public who still embraced the populism gained and hard won from the French Revolution. The ensuing *J'accuse* controversy lasted for years and culminated when Alfred Dreyfus was ultimately pardoned and released from confinement.

In the new media world, we do not often experience great journalists who exhibit the courage, integrity, and the thorough unbiased reporting of Émile Zola. In the 20th century, broadcast reporter Edward R. Murrow was legendary for his courageous in-the-trenches reporting from London during the bombings of World War II, and later his own "J'accuse" style of investigative coverage examining the ruthless tactics of Senator Joseph McCarthy helped to end one of the longest political witch hunts in American history. Then there was CBS newsman Walter Cronkite who shaped our views and opinions as a nation, from the Vietnam War to the end of the Reagan era.

Searching for Walter

I've been searching for Walter Cronkite, but I can't seem to find him. During the peak popularity of CBS News, Walter Cronkite reigned as "the most trusted man in America." It was Walter's authoritative persona that led us safely through the landmines of four major wars, the tumult of the 1960s, numerous assassinations, financial scandals, and the ushering-in of the Reagan era. He was there when the first man walked on the moon, and he was with us when Beatle John Lennon was gunned down in front of his apartment in New York City. Walter Cronkite was the kind of a guy Rudyard Kipling meant in his poem "If," when he wrote "If you can keep your head when all about you [people] are losing theirs."

Walter Cronkite kept a cool head. He represented integrity in journalism. When he said something, we believed him.

Through my work as a P.R. professional crafting case studies and testimonials, I've interviewed half a dozen key executives and asked them how they get their news. I thought they would tell me *The Wall Street Journal*, *The New York Times* or Twitter. I was shocked to learn that *The New York Times* was not on the top of their list. There was no pattern of how people got their news. These executives cited their primary sources of news as blog sites and content aggregators operating in niche markets. One executive received all of his news from a corporate in-house newsletter that aggregated the news based on what the company thought their employees should be reading.

Media has become so fragmented that as an industry and as a power it is broken. None of us are getting the same news because we choose to get bits and sound bites based on our interests instead of getting the most important news from a *single trusted new authority*. The problem with only focusing on news specific to our interests is that we have lost the ability to see the big picture. It's sort of like becoming so specialized in a niche that we lose our multi-disciplinary intelligence, the ability to weigh many sides of a story, and the power to know when to think and act decisively.

I have yet to find a news source that has the integrity of Walter Cronkite. So I'm still searching for him. One thing I know for sure, so far I haven't found him on Twitter and he's definitely not on Facebook. If you spot "Walter," then send me a text message. In the immortal words of Walter Cronkite, "And that's the way it is...."

Take another media icon: Rupert Murdoch. He is not Walter Cronkite. It's ironic that media mogul Rupert Murdoch has a challenge managing his own reputation in the press. The journalist Brooks Barnes, who covers media for *The New York Times*, wrote a piece about Murdoch that can only be described as *snarky*.[4] Barnes' lead for the story is a conversation he purportedly heard between two fifty-something LA matrons (who had had *work* done, he wryly observed) talking about how Rupert Murdoch was on the market again as a single man. Instead of journalism, Brooks' story sounds like negative spin, i.e., the bad stories high-priced P.R. professionals tell to discredit a foe.

It's hard to believe Barnes' journalistic source is derived by overhearing the conversation of two cosmetically altered women of a certain age. Talk about journalism, ethics, and credibility! Poor Rupert! His business scandals, family feuds and marital dirty laundry are splashed all over the many tabloids that he does not own, and especially in *The New York Times*, which at times, appears to be an arch rival to Murdoch's many media holdings. It's no accident that negative stories about Murdoch tend to be mightily diminished or nonexistent in *The Wall Street Journal* or on *Fox News* and emboldened in competing publications such as *The New York Times*.

Rupert Murdoch is a man who has amassed a mighty empire. He will always be able to get a good table in a restaurant, but he will never be loved by anyone. It is Rupert Murdoch's own fault for how he is perceived. His spin is about money and power. He never has a message about who he is as a person or how he creates value in the world. He is always positioned as having so much money that he will never be admired on his own merits as a man. Consequently, whoever feigns to love him, will always love his money too. When Jesus Christ said that a camel has a better chance of squeezing through the eye of a needle[5] than a rich man has of getting into the Kingdom of God, he was talking about Rupert Murdoch.

Why should anyone ever trust the media? On a very practical level, why should you ever trust any business relationship? And getting information from the media is most certainly a business relationship. The media makes money from advertising or selling sponsored content, which appears to be news but is paid editorial, commonly known as *pay for play*. The greater the number of viewers or readers, the more advertising revenue will be earned.

We don't have Edward R. Murrow or Walter Cronkite. Our most reliable news seems to come from Jon Stewart and Stephen Colbert, who are comic entertainers. In America, comedy is one of the few mediums where the truth can be told under the guise of being funny. If it's funny then it's okay to speak the truth. As a cultural phenomenon, it's sobering to think that the only way to have the privilege of telling the truth—without fear of retribution or of being ostracized and relegated as not important—is if we mask it in humor.

When we read, hear, or see any form of media, it is important to keep in mind that nothing is ever the way it seems. It always pays to probe beneath the surface to find out what is really going on. Always consider the source. And always consider why a story did get placed as news. Here is a story about how news was placed without a P.R. firm. In this example, the news fit with what was trending in the media.

Shortly after 9/11, on Tuesday, November 27, 2001, to be precise, I saw a photograph of my childhood best friend in *The New York Times* section: *A Nation Challenged*. Theresa Furrelle was not a mere friend or passing acquaintance. We had been best friends since the age of 13. Theresa's photo was large, a 5X7, and dead center in the middle of the obituary page of *Portraits of Grief*.

Only Theresa Furrelle wasn't dead; she was grieving. In the photo she was cradling the photo of a family member who had been a firefighter and had died in the Twin Towers. She was wearing dark sunglasses. Her brow was knitted in a terrible pain. Her mouth was fixed in the midst of a tremble.

When I saw my childhood friend's picture in the paper, I immediately assumed her loss was horrific. I called her that night to offer my condolences. Upon speaking to Theresa Furrelle though, I found out not only was the firefighter a distant relative (a somewhat removed relation of her fiancé), but she had only met him once.

Theresa's appearance at the funeral, dark hair, dark sunglasses, wearing all black, made a photograph memorable enough for *The New York Times* to transmit around the world. Theresa looked lovely, like the grieving widow who had lost her heart and would never love again. It helps that she also bears a startling resemblance to one of the greatest living screen legends of our times—Sophia Loren. In the P.R. industry, we call this a *photo op*. Theresa Furrelle didn't pay a P.R. person to get this photo op, which is the usual way photos, especially celebrity photos, get placed in the press. In this instance, *The New York Times* photographer thought that she was a great looking *Portrait of Grief*. It was easy to nab her photo. And the press likes *easy*. The media is a beast that just loves to be spoon fed the right photos, the right content, the right experts, to make filing a story on deadline, well, for lack of a better word, *easy*.

Now, I need to expound on one important aspect of *American Spin*: In the media, nothing is ever completely the way it seems. *The mission of the media isn't to transmit news per se; the mission of the media is to make money.* People must develop critical reasoning skills about what they see and hear in all facets of the media to protect their own interests so they can make informed decisions. It is important for people to understand who is behind the story that is being told. Trust what you see with your own eyes and hear with your own ears. You have instincts or an intuitive sense, so follow it and analyze it against independent data. Read a variety of sources. Get all sides of every story. Ask questions. Get answers. Think for yourself. Work for yourself. Trust no one but yourself. As the great American essayist Ralph Waldo Emerson said, "Trust thyself: every heart vibrates to that iron string. Accept the place the divine providence has found for you, the society of your contemporaries; the connection of events."

Astute journalists, editors, and producers who have genuine integrity and abide by a code of ethics no longer set the standard for what is reported in the press. Value can no longer be placed on journalistic ethics. Those days are gone. They died long before Jayson Blair[6] and others like him. In a 2013 in-depth report, *Amid Criticism, Support for Media's 'Watchdog' Role Stands Out*,[7] public evaluations of news organizations' performance on key measures such as accuracy, fairness, and independence remain mired near all-time lows.

For every great story that is placed in *The New York Times*, more often than not there is a *spinmeister* lurking behind the scenes who spun the story. For the uninitiated, a spinmeister is a P.R. professional who takes the essential facts to create a positioning or slant and then crafts this information to create a powerful story or *pitch* that is timely, compelling, relevant, and, in many instances, meaningful. In the increasingly complex world of communications, people of all ages need to develop the skills of a spinmeister. People need to approach P.R. as if it were an entrepreneurial pursuit. As our own spinmeisters, we must work as hard as entrepreneurs who are determined to build a business.

People also need to understand how spin is created to develop discernment for what is wholly true, half true, partly true, slightly true, and completely untrue, or a boldfaced lie. Consider Ralph Waldo Emerson and the great statements he sets forth in his landmark essay, *Self-Reliance*. "If we live truly, we shall see truly," he asserts. Emerson's *Self-Reliance* is the ultimate branding statement. A brand can't be sustained unless it is built on the truth. When a brand is built on truth, then spin can be used as an effective media tool to sway the hearts and minds of the masses. Although spin is a craft practiced by seasoned P.R. professionals, i.e., spinmeisters, the key for you to create successful spin is rooted in your persona. As we shall soon see, everyone has a brand persona that must be managed.

3

The True Measure of a Brand

A senior middle manager working for a Fortune 500 technology company called to learn if my P.R. firm could help reposition his professional brand. He had been with the same company for twenty years, but his most recent promotions had been lateral and he felt he would never be considered for the CEO slot. This company, similar to many others, does not promote a new CEO from within and instead recruits CEO candidates from outside the company.

His story was familiar to me. We do work with men and women who need to redefine their professional brands to gain entry to an exclusive club—the small cadre of CEOs, COOs, and CFOs who rotate from corporation to corporation with as much frequency as the childhood game of musical chairs.

All the branding and P.R. in the world isn't going change who he is and who he is not. As P.R. professionals, we're expert at staging perception. Sure we can make someone look good and sound good in the media, but we can't create a genuine leader.

Leadership is a function of your authentic persona. Branding is the implementation of your reputation. To assess your reputation, you have to ask questions, but you also have to be brutally honest with getting answers from people whom you know and trust.

What are others saying about you? Do you get positive feedback from those who are the closest to you? What do your spouse, siblings, significant others, and your children say about you? You can ask people who do not know you that well, but their responses are likely to be vague and superficial. And while it seems like a good way to assess your messaging platform and your public persona, people who do not know you that well will never tell you the truth.

You also have to assess how well you know yourself and not leave room for small white lies. Here are three quick questions.

Do people seek you out for both personal and professional advice and entrust you with their confidential information? Does your business network grow larger with little effort? Do people provide you with referrals, testimonials, and recommendations without you having to ask them to do so?

Through my many years of experience in P.R., here's what I've learned: Branding and P.R. are, to a large extent, completely inseparable. A brand is defined by everything you do, everything you say, and contrarily, your brand is also defined by what you do not do and what you do not say. Brand is not a distinctly different discipline from P.R. You are your own brand and your P.R. is *in action* every time you speak to a person. P.R. is everything you touch and everything you do. P.R. follows you everywhere from the minute you wake up in the morning to the moment you go to bed at night.

You as a brand need to create emotional relationships with people. Regardless of our gender, ethnicity, religion, politics, education, or economic status, people are emotional creatures and develop relationships with people whom they trust. You need to develop emotional connections and the best way to do that is by listening to what people have to say. Listen and listen well. It is amazing how, by listening intently, you will learn where the trouble spots are located. Learning about potential problems early in the conversation gives you the edge to find a better, quicker, smarter solution. When you truly listen to people, they will inevitably think of you as a gifted communicator, even when you have never even opened your mouth and they did all of the talking.

Who Needs to Use P.R. to Build and Manage a Brand?

Back in the day, intellectuals and academics shied from P.R. and there was a commonly held belief in these communities that utilizing P.R. tools was rather philistine and undignified. P.R. was something for the hoi polloi and not for the elite and credentialed. Now with the advent of social media, coupled with the complete meltdown of traditional press, it is more challenging than ever for intellectuals and academics to break through the clutter and to be seen and heard above the din. In the age of new media, only professionals who know how to utilize media to their best advantage will break through the clutter. For example, I have a client who is a world class oral surgeon with two advanced degrees and he has a prestigious teaching post at the University of Washington. And yet he must market himself because competitors who do not have nearly the credentials he has are aggressively marketing themselves, taking market share, and getting the patient referrals he should get. We are now living in a world where if academics do not effectively use P.R. tools they will be forgotten and left behind. It used to be publish or perish. In the age of new media, it is utilize the tools of P.R. or perish.

Creative professionals, business people, entertainers, and athletes—anyone who is in business today—must focus on using P.R. to build and manage a brand. Here is a comprehensive list:

1) Business people who want to build their reputations and prestige by having their clients and colleagues read about them in the press.

2) Authors who have written books and want to promote them.

3) Small business owners who want to promote and grow their businesses.

4) Owners of startup companies who want to establish a stake-in-the-ground.

5) CEOs and C-level executives who want to manage their reputations by getting press placement that will garner greater prestige and mindshare.

6) Job seekers who want to use the press as a way to get attention for their skills and talents.

7) People with middle management jobs who understand that their jobs do not define their brand and no job is secure. Branding is a way of securing opportunities for the future.

8) Creative professionals who want to get attention and leverage their creative portfolios in order to increase the number and quality of their clients.

9) Performing artists, athletes, and entertainers who want to get their name out there in order to get a higher profile and increased earnings.

10) Academics, students, and expertise seekers who want greater prestige for their fields of study in order to bolster their reputations and to increase opportunities for grants and job opportunities.

Whether you are a designer, an architect, an accountant, a lawyer, a comedian, or even a CEO, for you to have a major impact, you must have a strategy in place that will communicate your professional brand. First, you must define the *soul* of your brand. You need to understand your own history, your own core values, and who you really are before you begin communicating this essence to anyone else. If you don't know who you are, then how could anyone else possibly define the soul of your brand? Second, once you have a true understanding of the essence of your brand, then you can identify your position in the world. Third, you must understand the message that you want to send to the entire world.

We need to look at the most important element of branding, which is rooted in courage and the drive to be exceptional at what one does. Many people do not break through the clutter because they do not have the courage to dare to be exceptional. There is a shockingly high societal acceptance of mediocrity. Many people are afraid of taking an active stance to become truly unique individuals. With a measure of flawed thinking, many people are outer-directed and take a stance of pure conformity in order to avoid offending a group, a trend, or a person. Most people play it safe, staying in the middle, and avoid playing close to the *edge of the mat,* so they will be accepted by all and rejected by no one. The middle is not where you need to be. The middle is not safe. Stay in the middle and you will go nowhere.

The corporate middle manager who phoned me to rebrand himself as *CEO material* has been playing it safe and staying in the middle for his entire career, which is precisely why today he finds himself stuck in the middle with nowhere to move up. Even though he worked for a company like the long-term traditional *company man*, he had succumbed to having a corporate mentality instead of an entrepreneurial mindset. In the post-modern age, any person who does not develop a strong entrepreneurial mindset will not achieve his or her potential in business or in life. The entrepreneurial mindset requires us to be resourceful, creative and, when need be, rebellious to the cultural norms that dictate we must do things same old way.

How we often relinquish our autonomous and independent self in favor of conforming to the corporate mindset is well said in Ralph Waldo Emerson's grand essay *Self-Reliance*: "I am ashamed to think how easily we capitulate to badges and names, to large societies and dead institutions."

Despite the advent of mass communications, little has changed since Emerson's day. Corporate America is the reigning establishment and many of us play it safe by abiding to the corporate mindset and their rules and expectations for what is acceptable and what is not acceptable.

Are you willing to let someone else decide who you are? Or will you create your own role for how you will conduct yourself in life? The reality is no matter how safe an individual plays the game of growing a life, a business, and a career, there is no path safe enough. No matter how much an individual chooses to stay in the middle or how bland he creates his persona, he will inevitably offend someone and will risk losing the game anyway.

Your brand is your persona, your personhood; it is taking a public stance about who you really are. Oft-called a person's public image or a primary suit of color, persona is your signature, your face to the world. Succinctly put, everyone has to create a persona. Life is not kind to individuals who want to wallow in indecisiveness and do not want to make a decision about who they are. As a caveat, if you don't decide who you are, then others will make the decision for you. No one can afford to lose control over his or her own persona. It takes courage for individuals to be decisive about who they are and to act accordingly.

In 1856, John Stuart Mill said, "That so few now dare to be eccentric marks the chief danger of our time." What John Stuart Mill said over 150 years ago holds more true now than ever. This isn't to suggest that if we all behave in an odd fashion we will build better businesses and better communities. Daring to be eccentric is only the first step to gaining recognition for your brand.

A few years back, I spoke to a young architect who had a flair for P.R. and decided to get work by going to local street fairs, getting a booth, placing a tin cup on the table and offering architectural advice for 5 cents. Soon someone told the media about his tin cup and cheap advice. The press thought he was fun and upbeat—the perfect antidote to the barrage of grim economic news of joblessness and escalating debt. Soon the 5-cent architect was picked up in the local newspaper, and then he made it to NPR, numerous blogs, YouTube, and finally he was on to the big time—CNN.

We've witnessed publicity stunts from the Beatles' famous "Paul is Dead" campaign to accompany the release of *Abbey Road* to the Balloon Boy debacle. The *balloon boy hoax* happened on October 15, 2009, in Colorado, when Richard and Mayumi Heene allowed a helium-filled balloon to float away, claiming that their six-year-old son Falcon was trapped inside. It was soon discovered the couple had committed a hoax and they were charged with several violations and ordered to pay fines.

Publicity stunts will always be with us. They will get you attention and instant recognition, but they are no substitute for the steady, sustained devotion and discipline that it takes to build a solid, high quality brand. The 5-cent architect claimed he had a steady stream of work since his stunt. Now he claims to have another great P.R. stunt, but he is not sure he can get lucky twice, so he asked me what he should do. My advice to him and to anyone is: never rely on gimmicks. Instead, put in the time and do the hard work that it takes to build a successful brand. It's fine to be entrepreneurial about staging spin and to keep coming up with clever new ideas to get the word out about your work and expertise. However, it is critical to understand that it takes courage and hard work to sustain spin that is powerful enough to build a strong brand. Spinning should never come to stop. You need to spin with the passion that it will endure forever or until the last living person on earth can no longer remember your name.

Can Virgins Still be Queens? The Blended Approach to Spin

Queen Elizabeth I of England was a genius at P.R. and utilized a consistent entrepreneurial approach to spin throughout her reign. Daughter of the ill-fated Anne Boleyn, she was declared illegitimate after her mother was beheaded so that her father, King Henry VIII, could marry another woman and produce a male heir. In the 16th century, Elizabeth suffered from the equivalent of bad search rankings on Google—she was at the bottom of the chain of succession to the throne. Due to civil wars and premature deaths, Elizabeth came into power when she was 25 years old. England was a nation divided among the traditional Catholics, who still had ties to Rome, and the newly formed Anglican Church and Protestant insurgent faction. One false misstep from either side meant a quick trip to the Tower of London.

The most brilliant strategic move Elizabeth made was one of brand positioning. She donned the persona of the "Virgin Queen," or the Virgin Mary, Mother of Jesus Christ. By assuming this archetypal image, and surrounding herself with religious icons and symbols, Elizabeth could not be taken down by either the Catholics or the Protestants, both of whom adored and worshiped the Virgin Mary. Although both the Catholics and the Protestants vied for control of the nation, they stood united before the well-crafted image of the *Virgin Queen* who executed her brand with flawless precision. Instead of marrying and producing a male heir, she developed her Virgin Queen persona, successfully ruling a bitterly divided nation for 44 years with such cunning that she defeated the Spanish in 1588.

It's always good to use history to put P.R. into perspective. Had Elizabeth reigned today, she would have undoubtedly used many of the media tools now made available to all of us. She would have viewed the entire P.R. landscape and selected those tools to create a *blended reality* that best served her persona as the Virgin Queen.

What is *a blended approach to spin*? It is the seamless integration of media, both the old and the new. It means what you post on Pinterest may be slightly different than what you tweet about, but both messages are still true to your core brand regardless of whether you are the Queen of England or the owner of a shoe repair shop in Hoboken, New Jersey.

As for Elizabeth, one could easily see her in-depth feature story on the history of the Tudors in *The New York Times*, the photos of the wrecked boats from the Spanish Armada on her Facebook fan page and what she ate for dinner on Instagram. Although she would use all of the right tools to create her own *Blended Spin*, most of her conversations would still take place off-line behind the scenes, and not on a media platform for the entire world to see. Her LinkedIn might not include her true allies and influencers. One could hardly see Elizabeth tweeting *"off with your head"* or texting a mobile coupon *"Wanna win a trip for two to the Tower?"*

Using all of the social media platforms in the world is waste of time if you don't have a strong sense of strategy. To create a blended reality, you have to be certain of your positioning—of who you really are—and of the story you are telling to the world. Creating successful blended spin means knowing which tools to use and which ones you should never use. It also means knowing what message to share with each form of media, and of knowing when to do the deal behind closed doors and tell no one.

Brand is Not a Color

Branding and design professionals fervently believe it is great graphic design that builds a great brand, and they are correct to some extent, but it takes much more than color, layout, and graphics to create a brand that will stand the test of time. So I tend to distinguish building a professional brand from managing one's reputation. Once I was attending a business networking event, where I spotted a woman wearing a wide-brimmed red velvet hat. I am guessing her red hat was her way of making herself memorable. The woman in the red hat had attended a workshop called "black is not a color." The theme of the workshop was to teach professionals all about personal branding—how you have to stand out in order to get noticed. In a room full of crowded people, the red hat made it impossible not to notice the woman. But I never saw her. I only saw the red hat.

The Difference Between Personal Branding and Reputation Management
Your brand is what you stand for. Reputation management is everything you do and do not do to implement your brand. Personal branding is as simple and as shallow as wearing a red hat, signing up for a few events, and delivering an elevator speech. Reputation management requires a strategy as complicated as war. Reputation management *is exactly how* you build awareness for your brand. The key components of reputation management include strategic positioning, aggressive media relations outreach, building and maintaining a presence on select forms of social media, speaking at events and face-to-face networking, forming new business partnerships, giving back to the community through innovative volunteerism and pro-bono work, and generating positive word-of-mouth among people whom you know to be worthy of respect.

Reputation management is a daily grind, a discipline, and a strategy that reveals your true character and must be sustained for your entire professional life. True branding can only be implemented if you manage your reputation with hard work, determination, and individual productivity.

Managing your reputation is the only way to build your brand and establish your entire dossier of who you are and what you stand for. A dossier is typically an in-depth intelligence briefing, a descriptive litany telling everything about you, based on your complete biography of everything you have done. It's much more than your bio, résumé, CV, and references; your dossier is your comprehensive track record and even includes what your enemies say about you. Your dossier celebrates your strengths and minimizes or leverages your weaknesses. Your dossier is the truth and tells your story. It's like standing before God.

In the age of total transparency, if you want to build a career as a professional, you have to be prepared to manage your entire dossier. This means explaining why people, situations, and jobs spun out-of-control or did not always work out the way you wanted them to work. Managing your dossier means telling your story and showing the very essence of your character: your battles, your wins, your losses, your courage, and the steps that you took to reach for the next level.

I have often had professionals ask me: how can they get press? My response is: how about first doing the hard work to build a good name? Emerson's *Self-Reliance* is one of the most important branding statements ever written. "But do your work and I shall know you," he states. "Do your work, and you shall reinforce yourself." In *American Spin,* the primary tenet asserted is *Do good work. Be exceptional.*

Developing a professional brand means being exceptional enough to manage a strong reputation. Not everyone has the courage or the talent to dare to be exceptional. A strong professional brand isn't about being different from everyone else; it's about being better than everyone else.

Is "good enough" the new good? Has America become a culture of people who settle? Have we lowered our expectations? We accept bad or nonexistent customer service, lower school standards, and fewer services from the government despite bearing an increased tax burden. People seem indifferent to brand and act as if it will be taken care of automatically by managing a few simple things like hair color or wardrobe. Positioning and managing a professional brand is not about what you wear, or how you look, or even necessarily what you say.

An excellent reputation is built over time because you deliver what you said you would do, on time, and in a way that inspires everyone around you to do their best possible work. These are the common characteristics that make a great professional brand, a great entrepreneur, and a great leader.

Historically, having a great brand has always been important, but it wasn't known as a brand. Instead it was defined as one's persona. If you analyze history as a subject of enquiry, events and trends are influenced by the ruling personalities of the time period. From the Emperors of Rome to the current reign of celebrity CEOs, personalities have always been powerful enough to shape a country's core values and influence the way people lived, what they ate, what they wore, how they thought, and how they engaged in commerce. Persona is more than a predisposition granted by genetics or how an individual is reared. To some extent an individual's persona is how all others perceive that individual; it is the individual's public image—his or her face to the world.

Taking an active stance to build and manage a brand means people have to put in the time and hard work. There are no shortcuts. The word *industrious* has almost disappeared from our culture. Instead we have a culture where many people want to talk about their lifestyles and whether they can bring their dogs to work and want to know how much they can afford to spend on their next vacation. The reason why the word *industrious* has all but disappeared, and *integrity* is the buzz word *du jour* used by everyone from Banksters to Gangstas, is because anyone can feign integrity by claiming to have it. No one can fake the hard work it takes to be perceived as industrious.

Persona has much to do with who you really are. You cannot create a credible persona unless it is rooted in some truth. The truth ought to be rich, bold, and positive. And some positive truth is better than no truth at all. Spin advocates what is both true and what is positive about one's persona and diminishes the negative. Good spin can also take what is perceived to be negative and leverages it to be a positive attribute, a shtick. Shtick is Yiddish slang describing a characteristic, an attribute, or talent helpful in securing recognition or attention.

Hollywood film editor Lorne Morris was large, blow-hardy and a chronic stutterer. He worked so hard to become highly skilled as a film editor that his stuttering was leveraged to be an asset and a way to differentiate himself from all other film editors. Directors would ask for Lorne by referring to him as the *one who stuttered*. Lorne became one of the most highly sought after film editors in the commercial film industry.

When you are building your own brand, it is all about you, who you really are. It's okay to have thorns, i.e., a weakness or a flaw. In fact, no one is perfect and everyone has a major flaw. Identify your weakness and make it work for you. Position your greatest weakness as a great strength. The number one brand rule about weaknesses or flaws is that they ought to be used as a tool to identify and distinguish you, just so long as they never-ever stand in the way of your outstanding performance. Just like film editor Lorne Morris—he worked hard to become really good at his craft. His flaw became a unique identifier.

Everyone has a persona, and to some extent, everyone has a *shtick*. Shtick is the signature, the calling card that defines your persona. Much more than a single natural attribute or cultivated technique, one's shtick is the very essence of who a person is based on one's strengths and weaknesses, and it conjures the very essence of an individual personality. I take this concept one step further when I assert that in creating one's own persona, an individual can choose to command attention to her signature shtick. A shtick makes it easier for people to remember your persona. And it's not about donning a red hat.

Here are a few examples. Jacqueline Kennedy Onassis spoke in a whisper or a hushed little girl *sotto voce* voice to force people to listen more carefully and by doing so she shrouded herself in mystery. Perhaps she used this technique to diminish the fact that she was really shy or lacking in self-confidence. Michael Ovitz, ersatz Hollywood mogul before his fall, when he ran the once powerful Creative Artists Agency, had a penchant for speaking in a low understated voice, almost a mumble, and Chuck Yeager exhibited the same technique in his superb command as a pilot. Chuck Yeager's voice was cool no matter how much pressure he was under. If your shtick is good enough to strike a trend, it will be imitated by the mainstream. For years, Hollywood had a whole legion of agents who mumbled like Michael Ovitz. Most pilots exhibit grace under pressure in the cool tone and manner of Chuck Yeager. Think of Barbra Streisand; her big nose and big voice became her shtick.

The Killer Brand

Sometimes it is challenging to come up with a spin that is in total alignment with you and your business. Not so easy to do if your business is a new product app for an iPhone or software in the cloud. A story that is too zany or is concocted just to get attention can harm your business. Every so often, along comes a killer brand that achieves success, great revenue, and long-lasting fame because its story is the perfect fit with its fundamental business model.

Dave's Killer Bread is headquartered in Milwaukie, Oregon, and is owned in part by Dave Dahl along with his brother and his nephew. According to Dave, "I was a four-time loser before I realized I was in the wrong game. 15 years in prison is a pretty tough way to find oneself, but I have no regrets. This time around, I took advantage of all those long and lonely days by practicing my guitar, exercising, and getting to know myself—without drugs. To my utter amazement, I started liking what I was seeing. It's been said adversity introduces a man to himself and I found this to be true. If I had not suffered, I can safely assure you that you would not be reading this label on a loaf of my killer bread. A whole lot of suffering has transformed an ex-con into an honest man who is doing his best to make the world a better place...one loaf of bread at a time."

It helps that Dave Dahl looks like he can bench-press three times his burly bodyweight and he has the rugged looks of a rock star. But striking looks alone are never enough to catapult a person to fame. Bottom line, Dave's Killer Bread is a good product and a great story. The brand touches on a universal human condition: in life we all fail at something and sooner or later we all suffer enough to seek redemption and reinvent ourselves. Every human being has suffered from failure and has had to struggle to find a way back. Bottoming-out isn't only for junkies. Some people hit the wall because they lose money or a job. And others lose a great relationship. There are as many different ways to bottom out as there are ways we can emotionally connect with another human being who has failed, struggled, and paid the price to find the road back to redemption.

Dave's Killer Bread proves that it is still possible to launch a populist brand that resonates with everyone. It can be found in the small out-of-the way Mother Nature's health food store in Manzanita, Oregon, and in mega chain stores like Costco.

Leveraging a Weakness to Be a Great Strength

The true measure of a brand means your handicap, disability, or weakness can be leveraged to be a great strength. The Italian writer Umberto Eco noted that a rose called by any other name would still be a rose.[8] Unless it has been genetically altered, every rose has thorns. The rose without thorns lacks its immutable texture and its signature fragrance, and is, in a sense, no longer a true rose. In leveraging your own brand, you might consider how your own thorns can be leveraged to create a killer brand.

You may have seen Anthony Robles in the news. His bright yellow wrestling singlet shines, richly complementing his warm brown skin. He is the young man from Arizona State who won the 125-pound wrestling title at the 2011 NCAA Division I Wrestling Championships. What is notable about Anthony Robles—aside from the fact that he is young, handsome, and Hispanic—is his missing leg. Anthony Robles was born without a right leg. Not having a leg puts a whole different spin on being a champion wrestler.

The essence of Anthony Robles is about how he honed and perfected his strengths and minimized his weaknesses. Robles told an Associated Press Reporter, "My parents raised me to believe I could do whatever I set my mind to. I grew up thinking that way. I didn't think of my condition as something that could hold me back. I just thought this is how God made me and I'm going to make the best of it."

According to several reports, when Robles was a toddler he was fitted with a prosthetic leg. At age three, he tore off the leg and refused to wear it again.

Robles told the Associated Press, "Don't stay concerned with the negatives—what can hold me back, what my disadvantages are. I stay focused on the positive things—what I have, what I can do."

When asked about the challenge he faced as a wrestler, Robles said, "It doesn't have to be a missing leg, you could have any obstacle in your life. Whatever that is, you don't have to let that prevent you from doing things. You don't have to let the negativity of people or the doubters stop you from going after your dreams."

According to some sports observers, as a sophomore and junior, Robles tended at critical moments to forget the mantra "play your game" and did not lead with his own strengths, resulting in losses in the NCAA tournament. As a senior, he consistently transformed his physical disadvantage into a competitive advantage.

Robles made his opponents play to his great strength, which was his massively powerful upper torso. He had developed his upper body to become a formidable force to leverage—Robles is famous for his ability to swiftly lift and tilt his opponent's body in a single powerful sweep. Robles' disability became the source of his great strength. His upper body was larger than his opponents' because his weight did not include that of a second leg.

Anthony Robles put his school, Arizona State University, on the proverbial wrestling map. On March 19, 2011, in Philadelphia, before a crowd of 18,000 at the NCAA Division 1 Wrestling Championship, the 125-pound, 5'8" Robles overpowered defending NCAA champion Matt McDonough by a score of 7-1.

In fact, Robles' entire senior year at Arizona State had hit the mark of wrestling perfection—a 36-0 record.

Anthony Robles' missing leg may be a moot point. With or without a disability, Anthony Robles is a champion for all times, and serves as a lesson for us all. Robles maximized his strength and he stayed away from his weaknesses. He developed a strategic game plan and stuck to it. We all deal with our own frailties and weaknesses. But there is something to be gained by having a profound sense of knowing who you are. When you lead with your strengths, people rarely see your weaknesses. When you stand tall on one leg, no one notices the leg that is missing.

Anthony Robles worked hard to achieve his victory as an athlete. Celebrities come in many flavors so to speak, ranging from sports, arts, and entertainment to business, technology, and science… just to name a few disciplines. Celebrities are often perceived as being self-reliant—as having achieved the pinnacle of success, which represents complete autonomy. For those who are uninitiated into the realities of achieving great success, it might appear as though celebrities can do anything they want to do when it is the opposite that is true—with great notoriety comes even greater responsibility.

Experienced P.R. professionals strategically craft personae for their clients for a price. P.R. professionals manage their clients' reputations and spin carefully cultivated messages to all forms of the media. There is a high price to pay. Publicity services are expensive; P.R. is a luxury not everyone can afford. Most of the time, the public is not aware that what they are learning in the media about celebrities and other high profile individuals is based on pure spin. Consider the following celebrities: Martha Stewart, *America's domestic diva*; George W. Bush, *American cowboy*; Beyoncé, *America's sexy sweetheart*; Oprah, *America's uber-powerful woman of color*; Julia Roberts, *America's girl next store*; Jennifer Lopez, *America's spicy Latin pop diva*; Colin Powell, *American general*; Mick Jagger, *Rock and Roll's bad boy 'Sir Mick'*; Angelina Jolie, *Patron saint and sexy goddess;* Tom Cruise, *America's eternal boy ingénue.*

Madonna reinvents her persona on an average of a two year cycle: sex goddess, vamp, bad Catholic girl, the ultimate blonde victim Marilyn Monroe, the Geisha, the Latina, the uncrowned doyenne of British royalty, gorgeous dominatrix, mentor and high priestess to new girl singers on the way up. Madonna's shtick is taking female archetypal images and personifying them in her current music, choice of film roles, and the public portrayal of her lifestyle of the moment. Madonna has taken a unique talent for spotting trends in popular culture before they occur and capitalizing on them to the extent that she has built a wealthy empire.

The American culture reveres celebrities as setting the bar for self-reliance, or at least we project "self-reliance" onto celebrities. People live vicariously through celebrities because they are not strong enough to live their own lives. More than ever, ordinary people need to manage their persona deliberately and as if they are entrepreneurs building a business.

Carefully cultivating one's persona is certainly not the exclusive realm of the rich and famous. There is a simple difference: the rich can afford to pay professionals to execute their spin. Most people must rely on their own innate P.R. skills. Everyone must create his or her own persona. Teachers, carpenters, lawyers, students, construction workers, CEOs, accountants, hustlers, criminals, nuns, priests, day care workers, and farmers. Even dope dealers must manage their own persona. Witness *"El Chapo" Guzmán* ("Shorty" Guzmán) the former Mexican Drug kingpin of the Sinaloa Cartel that is the #1 supplier of illegal drugs to the US Tales of El Chapo's violent exploits, extradition, escapes, and recaptures have become legendary. No one is exempt from having to create his or her own persona. Individuals from all walks of life, lawful or otherwise, must build a brand and manage their reputation.

Ask yourself, "Who am I?" The core of one's persona stems from the essence of how a person presents his or her self to the world. What do you want the world to know about you? What do you stand for? What have you done? What do you believe in? Whom do you trust? What experiences have shaped your life? What do you choose to hold private and sacred to yourself? What aspirations define who you are on the road to becoming? Don't tell me you don't know who you want to be when you grow up. Grow up deciding who you are, what you want to say to the world, and how you want to say it!

Don English is among my favorite people. (Don English is not his real name and is being used to protect his identity.) What fascinates me about Don is his persona exudes the innocence of a curious child. Hardly a kid, Don English is an accountant pushing fifty. He asks philosophical questions, the tough questions. He probes the financial issues of our times (the 2008 financial collapse, the changing job market, high unemployment, and the national deficit), as if he is seeking answers for his own life's journey. He always expresses confusion as to why people take advantage of others in business and cause harm.

While Don is a CPA by profession, he professes to have the soul of an artist. Listen to his messaging… He claims he could never cope in the competitive corporate environment of one of the big accounting practices. In his small solo boutique practice he refuses to implement OTB (off the books) "creative accounting." He knows how to calculate complex spreadsheets, but he claims not to understand the realities of business, which are rooted in power and greed. He would never cheat the IRS or mislead his client's investors. And when he is asked to cook the books, Don always refuses. In line with Don's total nature of humility, this man is good-natured even about the personal tragedies that have beset him.

Don English's persona is very much like Prince Myshkin, the main character in Fyodor Dostoevsky's classic book *The Idiot*. Prince Myshkin has a persona that exposes the spiritual emptiness and moral corruption of the world. According to Dostoevsky, his aim was "to depict the positively good man." Dostoevsky went on to say: "There is nothing more difficult than this in the world, especially nowadays."

The Jesus-like Prince Myshkin is honest, truthful, and innocent, just like Don English. The inherent nature of the human being has not changed since the late 19th century when Dostoevsky wrote *The Idiot*. If anything, only the speed of our technological advances in communication has intensified our knowledge of our vacant spiritual conundrum.

Don told me he owned a Mercedes for six months and all that happened was he attracted hordes of strange opportunistic women, telemarketers, and salesman who wanted to date his portfolio instead of him. He claims most of the world doesn't have time for his humanity. He gives the appearance of bumbling his way through life, but in reality he is making a ton of money.

Don English is spewing good spin. He is sending the message to the world that unlike other accountants, he is honest, forthright, and someone to be trusted with your most valuable asset—your money. Being an idiot is Don's persona and it works for him. He guards it carefully. I know if I retain his services he will do honest work. He wouldn't do anything to jeopardize what I believe to be true about him.

The real self, who you really are, and your face to the world, how you actually present yourself, ought to be indistinguishable from one another. Otherwise you would be living a lie. First and foremost, you must decide who you really are. Then it is up to you to live up to your own standard. Carefully consider every word you speak and every action you take. These are the elements that will always define your persona, not just who you really are but who people think you are. Your persona belongs to you. You are the one who controls what people will believe about you. Your words, your actions; ultimately you are responsible.

A persona must be well thought out. If people detect you are making up something about yourself that is patently untrue, they will instinctively go after you and unravel your hard earned reputation. As a caveat, it is important not to allow others to create your persona. You may run into people who tell you who they think you are. In this case, what they are telling you is not designed for your greater self-awareness or to enhance your personal growth. Instead what they are saying about you is untrue. They are labeling your actions or describing you in their own words to suit their own whims. When another person has defined you against your wishes, you can bet they are trying to gain the upper hand and assert control over you.

In Hollywood, the notion of persona is even more extreme than in the non-entertainment world. I have often heard top stars complain of not receiving accolades for their best work and then receiving awards for work they found to be mediocre. An associate of mine, screenwriter Clay Frohman, who wrote the screenplay for the Nick Nolte, Gene Hackman film, *Under Fire*, understood the power of image in Hollywood. Clay said the most important lesson he had learned in Hollywood: "Never believe them when they tell you, 'you're great' and never believe them when they tell you, 'you're lousy.'" The way an audience perceives you may have little to do with one's true persona, and that is a major problem. One that must be managed.

No matter what field you are in, when it comes to building your brand, you are an entrepreneur; your persona is a business, an entity people will want to take stock in. You are creating a public trust. What can people count on? What will people believe about you? Who cares about love and adoration! Will people trust you? Will people respect you? When I tell you to carefully consider every word you speak and every action you take, it is because everything you do is an extension of your brand.

The finest spin is included in the stories that are told about people who are known as great leaders, experts, athletes, business people, entertainers, or celebrities—those individuals who are perceived as being influential. The creation of one's persona is not an accident and it is much more than a personal choice. The creation of a persona means doing the work that defines who you are, and more importantly it means everyone (and that means anyone who matters) knows about you and your work.

The Iconic Brand

One of America's founding fathers, Benjamin Franklin, is known for being a brilliant statesman and an arbiter of public opinion. More importantly, Benjamin Franklin is known for the many things he accomplished as an inventor, scientist, writer, publisher, printer, politician, entrepreneur, and raconteur. However, he is not known for being a master of spin. And yet he was a brilliant mastermind who wove tales about himself, those issues of the times that he deemed to be important, and especially about the birth of the United States of America. There is no doubt that Franklin was a master of spin. His first and primary occupation was as a writer, publisher, and printer—he knew how to get the word out about his work and his persona.

Franklin became the first to publish a novel in America in 1744 when he reprinted *Pamela*, by Samuel Richardson. If he lived in the 21st century, Ben Franklin could have easily invented a device like the iPad and instead of giving content away for free, he would use it as a tool to make money for his publishers and authors. Franklin wasn't a proponent of giving away content for free. He made a small fortune from the sales of *Poor Richard's Almanac*. The ease with which we can now publish is the same as it was in America in Ben Franklin's 18th century. Franklin would write an article in the morning, send it off to the printer in the afternoon and by nightfall, his work would be distributed to every coffee house and tavern in Philadelphia. By the time Franklin was forty, he turned his work over to his foreman David Hall, who then became his partner. Franklin still owned half the printing business and netted a substantial annual income. Eventually, he retired from printing, publishing, and bookselling so that he could devote his time to scientific research and public service.

Through the artful cultivation of his communication about his work and beliefs, Benjamin Franklin became the embodiment of the people's brand and the principles he stands for: freedom, independence, self-autonomy, hard work, and innovation. Franklin's core principles have come to represent the core values for American culture. Franklin was a champion of practical intelligence and he also stood for frugality, discipline, and resourcefulness. If he came back to live in the 21st century, one could hardly imagine him maxing out his Visa card at the *Prada* store on Madison Avenue in New York City. He just didn't stand for lavish spending and living beyond one's means. Even though he could have easily afforded *Prada* (Franklin was a wealthy man) he wouldn't have worn a brand that countered who he was.

While much is made of Franklin's inventions, explorations, and political influence, everyone fails to mention one of his finest talents of all—he was really good at P.R. That is why he was able to get distributed so quickly in the coffee houses and the taverns. He knew all the right networks. Ben Franklin wasn't about selling books. Ben Franklin knew how to build a brand. And we all know that without his behind-the-scenes efforts with the French, we might not have won the war against the British. Ben Franklin was one of America's most influential founding fathers. But think of how his brand has endured far beyond the coffee houses and taverns of Philadelphia. Ben Franklin's colorful life, his legacy, his brand, is on our money: the fifty cent piece and the hundred dollar bill. His name is on warships. He is the namesake for many towns, counties, educational institutions, and companies. More than two centuries after his death, his brand has endured and achieved the status of a cultural icon.

Iconic brands, using Benjamin Franklin as an example, stay relevant for centuries for three reasons: networking, reinvention, and P.R. First, Franklin was a master of networking and spent a lifetime forming strategic alliances, partnerships, and making new business contacts that created an intricate, global web of interconnected relationships. Second, Franklin was a master of constantly reinventing himself: author, printer, publisher, scientist, inventor, diplomat and statesman, and businessman. Franklin was the quintessential entrepreneur who explored and successfully exploited new business opportunities everywhere he traveled. The third reason why Franklin's legacy endured is because his persona was associated with countless numbers of organizations, academic institutions, government entities, businesses of all sizes and types, who have had a vested interested in keeping his brand alive. It is no accident that Benjamin Franklin remains a household name after all this time. The primary tool used to keep a brand alive is through using P.R.; it's called Dead P.R.

A business colleague asked me whether I do P.R. for dead people. Doing P.R. for the dead is the same as doing P.R. for the living. There is one advantage, however; a dead client can't do or say something stupid. Any organization or entity bearing Franklin's name will always cite its namesake on billboards, in advertising, in press, brochures, and websites and on social media. As long as these institutions promote themselves, the name of Benjamin Franklin[9] will never be forgotten. Once a brand name has gained mass adoption, from universities to municipalities, the brand gains traction on its own recognizance and achieves a powerful momentum.

Dead P.R.

Ever wonder why dead celebrities keep turning up in the news? Ever wonder why Elvis Presley and Marilyn Monroe just won't go away? Families, trusts and estates, and foundations pay P.R. people a lot of money to keep their brand legacies alive. The estates and families of dead celebrities have reason to keep resurrecting the names of the deceased. It's called *Brand Equity*. There is a lot of money and new licensing deals yet to be made when a brand is kept alive by P.R. people who have been hired to pitch and place new stories about the same old thing.

Back in 2000 when I was VP of Communications for one of the first digital publishers, PublishingOnline, I went to London to meet with Glidrose Productions, which held the rights to *James Bond*. Most people don't know why James Bond kept coming back long after James Bond's creator, Ian Fleming, was dead. Ian Fleming was from a wealthy English banking family who recognized the inherent long-term value in the James Bond brand and was able to invest in the brand to keep it alive.

Ian Fleming wrote twelve novels and two collections of short stories. After Fleming's death, the celebrated British literary author Kingsley Amis was paid to write one Bond book under a pseudonym (Robert Markham). British literary giant John Gardner took on the Bond assignment and wrote fourteen novels and two film novelizations. Chicago-based Raymond Benson became the fourth official writer of the James Bond 007 novels. Raymond felt that after six original novels, three film novelizations, and three short stories, he needed to do something new and today is successfully building his own brand as an author.

According to Benson, "I got the [James Bond] job mainly because Mr. Peter Janson-Smith and the people at Ian Fleming Publications Ltd. (back then it was called Glidrose Publications) had assisted me with my non-fiction, encyclopedic work, *The James Bond Bedside Companion*, which was first published in 1984. They liked the book and figured I knew the Bond universe. Which was true. We stayed in touch through the late eighties and early nineties, and then in late 1995 I got the call from Peter, asking if I'd like to take over from John Gardner, who was retiring from the gig."

The brand legacy of James Bond has endured long after Ian Fleming's death because his family recognized the financial rewards that would be reaped by continuing to promote the books, movies, and the creative works attached to the James Bond brand. Dead P.R. notwithstanding, if Ian Fleming hadn't done the hard work to create James Bond in the first place, there wouldn't be a brand worthy of promotion.

Achieving a strong brand doesn't happen by accident. Ralph Waldo Emerson said, "And we are now men, and must accept in the highest mind, the same transcendent destiny; and not minors and invalids in a protected corner, not cowards fleeing before a revolution, obeying the almighty efforts and advancing on chaos and the dark." What Emerson suggests is we need to do the hard work it takes to fulfill our destiny. If Emerson had lived today, he would have been acutely aware that the extent that we shape our own destiny is rooted in the work we choose to do to build a strong brand. We are responsible for our own brand destiny.

The most important aspect of spin is managing your professional reputation by developing a strong persona. If you don't have a strong brand, no one will believe your spin, even when it is the truth. It is not enough to only build a brand but the owner of the brand must ensure that is constantly expanding. The mission is powerful and unstoppable—to grow colleagues and contacts by constantly enlarging the brand's audience. Most important of all, the owner of the brand must create the perception that the brand is creating value. Bottom line: Your brand must create value or it does not stand a chance of sustaining success.

Carving out a credible persona is essential to everyone. By managing your persona with an entrepreneurial mindset, your best work is grounded in cold-hearted practicality. Ralph Waldo Emerson wrote in *Self-Reliance*, "Most of our jobs, our work, our endeavors are inherently wired to prevent us from becoming great." Emerson was a champion of the entrepreneurial mindset and he understood what it takes to be innovative enough to build a business. These same principles—derived from having an entrepreneurial mindset—also apply to the active building of a brand. When describing the work of the entrepreneur, Emerson wrote, "He has not one chance, but a hundred chances." You need to take all of these chances.

4

Messaging and the North Star

From the perspective of a wily P.R. practitioner, propaganda is actually a *messaging platform*. Individuals, institutions, businesses, governments, and people use a platform (propaganda) composed of key messaging statements to communicate an idea or a doctrine to sway the hearts and minds of the majority. Propaganda or the messaging platform is the set of facts that are conveyed in a story. What facts are left in and which facts are left out of the story? What facts are embellished or emphasized and which facts are relegated to be so trivial that they are not worth mentioning at all? Those facts that are selected become the messaging platform or propaganda. The angle or positioning from which the story is told is *the Spin*. And the story itself is a tale, a creative concept, a yarn, and it must strike an emotional chord with the audience. The listener or recipient or audience of a story is very likely to be left with the impression that the storyteller has intended all along.

Messaging as Constant as the North Star

Messaging must be as unfailingly consistent and in its consistency as constant as the North Star. This isn't to suggest that messaging must be simple. Great messaging can even contain paradox or opposing sets of beliefs that create dynamic tension. For example, Pope Francis travels the world commingling with the common folk with every smile and ceremonial *laying of hands* captured on film, in video, and digitized across all forms of media for the world to see. The Pope has stated in numerous press conferences that women could have a greater role in the church.

But the Pope has also made it abundantly clear that only men can be priests.[10]

The message is one and the same: Women have a place in the church so long as they do all the grunt work, but they will never have any stature, a title, prestige or power.

Spin isn't based purely on fact, but also contains enough of the emotional context to move people. Pope Francis sitting down to have lunch with low-level Vatican workers isn't a story unless it is told within its emotional context. In the short time since he donned the sceptre, the Pope has spent his time making close personal connections with people from all walks of life, behaving as if he is Jesus walking among the crowded streets of Jerusalem, blessing the sick and uplifting the hearts of the poor. Pope Francis is the first Holy See to grace the cover of *Rolling Stone* magazine.[11]

Good spin is artful, clever, and above all, it must be plausible. Good spin told and sustained over time builds up to a "reveal" so the audience can draw their own conclusion. The Pope sitting down to have lunch with Vatican workers isn't of itself extraordinary. It is the consistency of the Catholic messaging that is compelling. Each successive story showing the Pope ministering to ordinary people becomes a layering of stories that builds to a crescendo and delivers the following message: Pope Francis cares about all human beings and ministers to them no matter where he finds them, even if some of them are women.

Yo Hillary! What's Your Message?

Having name recognition doesn't mean you've built a brand that connects with your audience. Take Hillary Rodham Clinton. Everyone knows who she is, but no one knows what she stands for, i.e., her brand is lackluster and she doesn't have a message. Examining Hillary Clinton's brand has less to do with her career as a high profile politician and much more to do with what happens when you put yourself out there in front of the media and you don't have a message.

In Ken Auletta's article, "The Hillary Show" in the June 2, 2014, issue of *The New Yorker*[12], he suggests that Hillary Clinton's tenuous relationship with the media has been less than ideal and at times downright contentious. He gives credible evidence from right wing press, *The Weekly Standard* and *Free Beacon*, to show exactly how Hillary has been vilified, attacked, and ridiculed in the media. And while Mr. Auletta presents a story that is compelling and entertaining, he is fundamentally missing a major point—Hillary Clinton is a high profile politician who lacks a message. And when you lack a clear message, the media will make up one for you.

Examine Hillary's brand from the most rudimentary of all PR principles: What are the three core attributes that define Hillary Clinton's brand? *Ambition. Competence. Bill's Wife.* These three attributes are so powerful that if one were taken away, Hillary would cease being Hillary. It is the combo of three attributes that define her brand. Take away any of her core brand attributes—Ambition, Competence, and being Bill's Wife—and she wouldn't be slated to run for President in 2016.

Noting one of Hillary's core attributes as being Bill's Wife is not meant to slam her seasoned political acumen, inherent leadership ability and her formidable political experience. It is a matter of perception. We perceive Hillary Clinton as the wife of Bill—two for the price of one.

Forget about Bill for a minute; if the American public and the media only perceived Hillary as *Ambitious* and *Competent*, these facts alone should win her the Presidency. In America today, being competent is no small thing. From the C-suite to the ground floor of clerical workers, competence is sorely lacking in all industries and sectors regardless of the size of the organization. Hillary Clinton is undeniably competent. Hillary has gravitas and she has earned our respect. She is worth voting for simply because she is eminently qualified and highly competent.

And yet the question must be asked: What does she stand for?

On the Weekly Standard Morning Joe show[13], co-host Mika Brzezinski challenged Sen. Tim Kaine (D., Va.) to describe Hillary Clinton's potential message for her presidential run in 20 seconds and he was unable to do so. "The message is she has the best experience, both domestically and internationally," he said.

"She has got the accumulated backbone, wisdom, judgment, scar tissue from a long period in public life to be the best President of the United States beginning in 2017."

Still, Hillary Clinton doesn't have a message.

If one of Hillary Clinton's supporters couldn't articulate her message, then how could the rest of us figure it out? Lacking a message has made Hillary Clinton fodder for many other media outlets that are not right wing. The Major broadcasters: NBC, ABC, CBS, PBS, NPR, CNN, MSNBC, CNBC; and top-tier press, such as the *Huffington Post*, the *New York Times,* and the *Washington Post*; and even liberal publications such as the *New Republic* are not reticent in their criticism of Hillary Clinton.

Fox Business Network anchor and commentator Neal Cavuto proclaimed that "men wouldn't vote for Hillary because she reminds them too much of their nagging wives." Cavuto's snarky quip says more about how Cavuto communicates his own brand to his audience than it does to define the message of Hillary Clinton.

Even Gloria Steinem, who is a staunch Hillary supporter, communicates her own powerful *feminist* brand and mission to amplify the voice and power of women and how women are perceived in the media. Steinem asserts, "Journalists affix adjectives to female candidates—shrill, pushy, aggressive, ambitious, divisive, bossy—that they don't apply to males." While Steinem is accurate in her assessment of the bastion of journalists who bash Hillary Clinton, the gender issue doesn't explain everything.

If our perception of Hillary Clinton is maligned by her gender, then why aren't more women supporting her? In 2008, primary polls showed a majority of high-earning, educated and powerful professional women voted for Barack Obama and not Hillary Clinton. It's not the gender issue that is the only threat to Hillary Clinton. It's also about her brand and her inability to communicate a message that demonstrates a clear and purposeful vision.

Viewing Hillary Clinton through the narrow lens of gender invites the obvious comparison to two other current female politicos. Former Governor of Alaska Sarah Palin and

Massachusetts Senator Elizabeth Warren, both of whom embody
their brands, one far to the right, the other left, clearly articulate
a message that has the power to inspire.

Sarah Palin recently said, "May that love of liberty burn in our
hearts and renew our commitment to restore and preserve all that is
good and strong and true about America." And she urged Americans
to remember the words of Thomas Jefferson and Ronald Reagan.

Elizabeth Warren stands for full throttle anti-Wall Street
liberalism. She delivers the populist message that hard work
and true grit will get people what they want, and if it doesn't,
she will fight to get it for them. Elizabeth Warren's message is
impassioned and clear: She will reinstate the American Dream
for the American people.

Sometimes Not Having a Message Can Be the Message

Sometimes not having a message can be well-thought-out
strategic positioning. For whatever reason, Hillary Clinton
chooses to rely on the power of her persona instead of crafting
a messaging platform that connects with her many multiple and
diverse audiences.

Standing for nothing and just being plain Hillary (Ambitious,
Competent, and Bill's Wife) might be part of her game plan.
She has a tangled web of relationships with global leaders,
financiers, money brokers who are the bedrock of a highly
complex financial network. Many of Hillary Clinton's most
powerful allies possess enormous amounts of cash made from
dealings on Wall Street and they were extremely instrumental
in limiting the reach of the Dodd-Frank Wall Street Reform and
Consumer Protection Act, the financial reform measure Obama
signed in July of 2010.

If Hillary articulated a message that had a strategic vision,
she could accomplish a turnaround—the return to the concept
that an American Dream is accessible to everyone. She could
be the next FDR and launch a Works Progress Administration
(WPA) that puts America to work to rebuild our deteriorating
infrastructure. If Hillary had a vision and stood for something,

we would believe her. We would believe that she could do it. After all, she is competent, ambitious, and Bill's Wife.

Lacking a powerful message can cause Hillary Clinton to lose the Presidency—again, but she doesn't really have a choice. Hillary Clinton doesn't have the freedom to communicate a powerful brand message that evokes vision, clarity of purpose, and a moral compass for the future. She's not in a position to address why the poor get poorer, the rich get richer, and the middle class get squeezed trying to make ends meet. By communicating a powerful message that addresses the controversial issues of economic parity, she could alienate some of her largest political donors and supporters. She's already done the deal with the devil and there's no turning back.

If You Don't Have a Message What Can Happen?

Everyone must manage his or her own reputation. If you plan to build a high profile reputation for yourself, you will need to not only have a message, but you will have to spend time managing your messaging. You can ignore the caveat that everyone must manage his or her own reputation. But by doing so, you will ensure that sooner or later you will be embroiled in a situation that requires crisis management, which is often painful, embarrassing, and costly.

One of my chief frustrations as a P.R. professional is when I've been hired by a client who claims to have been thinking about P.R. for years and has firmly decided that *Now* is the time to launch a campaign. *Now* is the operative word here. Usually by the third week of engagement, I learn that the client is in deep distress, the business is falling apart, and there is scandal threatening to erupt everywhere. This is not an ordinary P.R. initiative, it's crisis communications, and nine times out of ten, it could have been avoided if the client had been conducting pro-active P.R. long before a crisis erupted. Usually, they want me to fix the problem overnight, and they hold my feet to the fire when I cannot walk on water. These types of clients are like the Roman Emperor Nero, and they deserve to have a brand that's under fire.

The story of the Roman Emperor Nero playing the fiddle while Rome burned is untrue. For one, the fiddle would not be invented for another 1,500 years. Another more important reason why the story is untrue is Nero wasn't even in Rome at the time the fire broke out. He was vacationing in his summer home close to the Mediterranean Sea in Anzio. When Nero learned that all of Rome was burning to the ground, he and his guards and staff rode all night on horseback to get back to Rome. As they entered the city, it was clear that the devastation was everywhere. Nero and his team put in a valiant measure to put out fires and to rescue injured citizens. One report depicted Nero as heroically covered with soot, and running into a burning building to save a family. In the fire's aftermath, he opened his imperial gardens to serve those who had been left homeless by the fire and pledged to rebuild the city.

How Nero came to personify a madman gleefully playing a fiddle while the city burned to the ground is a tribute to what happens when you've already been branded as a bad guy. Nero was reportedly vain, shallow, and manically egotistical, and he had as many enemies in the Roman Senate, the Praetorian Guards, and Roman landowners as he had in his own family. Nero killed many people including his own mother, Agrippina. And while killing your mother is admittedly a huge crime, Agrippina was not an ordinary mother. She was a royal monster, who had left her own trail of destruction and had conspired to have her son murdered.

Nero could have softened his image a little if he had a handle on extolling what he did that was noble and good. If only he had done a little P.R. and had done something to manage his reputation with strong messaging, then history could have taken a different twist. Operative rule to live by: when you have a reputation as a bad guy, people will blame everything on you, whether you did it or not.

Take Marie Antoinette, who was in the wrong place at the wrong time. The ill-fated French Queen often indulged in excess and finery while the peasants starved and had no flour for bread, but she never said, "Let them eat cake." The oh-so-terrible quote was attributed to her by a French journalist.

Managing one's reputation is something we all need to do, especially when we've been extraordinarily bad. In school, we all knew the kid who was always in trouble and who often ended up taking the blame even when he had done nothing at all. Become lax with managing your reputation and you can become a scapegoat for all the ills in the world. No one should have to bear the burden for all the world's troubles, even if you have been very bad. Managing your reputation may be one of the most important things you will ever do. The only thing worse than overexposure and doing too much P.R. is to not manage your reputation at all.

Brand as Constant as the North Star

How do you implement strong messaging? Stay on course, don't let anything get in your way and, metaphorically speaking, keep traveling north. When I talk to people who want to use P.R. to manage their reputations, inevitably I hear that they are doing one or two things, but they don't seem to have a message, and without a message, they will not break through the clutter. To implement your message, you need to do a whole lot of things in a disciplined way (a fully integrated program that includes P.R. tools specific to media relations, social media, and business networking) and sustain this activity over a period of time.

The mightiest ship of the 20th century, the Titanic, was destroyed when it hit an iceberg. In the blockbuster film *Titanic*, Jack Dawson is a near-penniless artist who in a card game won a third-class ticket on the ship. He gets a free ride on the Titanic. Some prize. He saves socialite Rose DeWitt from distress and the two begin a relationship. Except Rose is riding first-class and Jack is riding steerage. *We all know what happened to Jack Dawson.*

Do you want to ride steerage on the Titanic or do you want to do the hard work that it takes to build a brand? One reason why the rich prevail prominently and consistently in the press is because they can pay P.R. professionals to create their messaging, do their brand-building, and manage their reputations. As an individual without vast financial resources, you will have to create your own messaging and do your own P.R. There is never any substitute for doing the hard work it takes to create solid messaging. While P.R. is the most entrepreneurial way to build a brand, crafting great messaging is tricky. There are many elements that must be considered. Your messaging must be cleverly crafted to show the value that your brand is creating in a way that resonates with your audience. The primary tool involved in spreading your message is by using the media as a conduit for mass communication. Before you even think of getting news coverage, you have to develop strong messaging that is a logical extension of your brand persona and, at the same time, seductive enough to be heard by your audience.

5

Romancing Your Audience

For the past eight years, I have passionately pursued a hobby as a dancer. Ironically, when I'm training in ballet, I embrace great tenets about business, branding, and how to connect with an audience. One Saturday I made the following observation. I was practicing turns in the largest studio at Pacific Northwest Ballet (PNB). The ballet studio was large and easily accommodated a class of fifty students. Inside turns, outside turns, arabesque turns, and whipping into a wild torrent of chainé turns.

People passing in the hall often stopped to look in through the windows. Parents, spouses, friends and lovers, other dancers, instructors—the onlookers could be anyone. Through the glass this one woman was watching me. I felt annoyed and secretly wished she would go away. I wasn't there to perform for her. I was there for me.

I wanted my audience of one to leave.

Suddenly I thought how foolish I was being. If I wanted to *exercise* and not be seen, I could go to the gym and ride a stationary bike while I read a book. Ballet is a performance art, not a spin class at the gym. In the ballet studio, flattering lighting and glass surrounded me; mirrors and windows were everywhere and my body was adorned in a shiny leotard and ripped tights. I had intentionally placed myself in the optimal position to attract an audience the same way many individuals are using social media to promote themselves.

While there is a powerful argument to be made that anyone can use the media to get the word out to create awareness for one's persona, most communication is little more than idle banter. In the current state of media, both legacy media and social media, there is an avalanche of clutter that makes it a challenge for any one individual to elevate his persona above the din. Many people are getting lost in the clutter. And while having wealth at one's disposal to buy media attention ensures a greater chance of gaining recognition, the reality is anyone can break through the clutter to reach the right audiences. If the reality is that anyone can break through clutter by using free P.R. tools like social media, then why aren't more people achieving celebrity status or getting recognition for their accomplishments?

One reason why people are not heard is because they consistently devalue or overlook their audience. Many people do not even know who their audience is. How often do we invite an audience to the table and offer them nothing? By writing blogs, emails, articles, books, and posting all over social media, and shouting as loud as we can, we have all become performers. Even though we've invited an audience to the table, we really don't care about them. We only want them to buy, sell, like, follow, or become fans. It's sort of like Sally Field shouting at the top of her lungs, "You like me. You really like me!"

We're communicating all over the place, but no communication is actually taking place. We're all guilty of much more than putting on a bad performance. We're being bad communicators.

Peter Drucker once said, "There is no sound in the forest unless someone can hear it. It is the recipient who communicates. The so-called communicator, the person who emits the communication, does not communicate. He utters. Unless there is someone who hears, there is no communication. There is only noise. In communicating, whatever the medium, the first question has to be is this communication within the recipient's range of perception? Can he hear it?"

Communication takes place when you are communicating to an audience that might actually want to receive what you have to offer. Look at it from your audience's perspective and ask yourself: What's in it for them?

Where is your audience's point of pain or point of passion? What will move them, touch them, and captivate them? You have to care why they would be interested in what you have to offer.

Creating the greatest messaging in the world is insignificant if you have not identified the audience who might be interested in listening to what you have to say. Most important of all, consider telling a clever story or two. Actually, considering telling a clever story or two is an understatement. You need to spin great stories for the rest of your professional life. You need to build a brand legacy.

Scheherazade: How to Save Your Own Head

From the Arabian nights comes the tale of Scheherazade. She had a once-in-a-lifetime opportunity to marry the King of Persia. This King, however, had been stung by a past wife who cheated on him. With the vengeance of a powerful man scorned, the King each night took a new bedmate from among the fairest virgins in his kingdom. When dawn arrived, the King ordered his newest consort to be put to death by a swift beheading.

Along comes Scheherazade. During her night with the King, she begins telling him a story. As dawn approaches, her story is not over; it's a cliffhanger. The King, drawn in by her unfinished story, keeps her around until the next night, the night after, and the night after that, until Scheherazade is there in his bed chamber for One Thousand and One Arabian Nights. That's nearly three years. By that time, Scheherazade wins not only the King's heart, but also his trust. You know the rest: They marry, produce three sons, and live happily ever after.

Scheherazade had more than 140 characters to weave a powerful tale. And here is where the power of good storytelling is crucial. If you haven't been telling a good story all along, then no one is going to recognize if there is any substance behind your tweets, posts, and all your prattle on social media.

People and businesses of all sizes need to think of themselves as more than just churners of content; they need to think of themselves as storytellers who are weaving a succession of powerfully rich tales. To do the opposite—to publish junk, everyone else's quotes, mindless chatter, and boring "how-to" lists and guides—will not keep you inside of the King's bedchamber. The lack of a good story will cost you your head.

It took Scheherazade nearly three years of telling riveting tales to win the King. She told stories that mattered to him, but she also told stories that entertained him and kept him on the edge for one more night. Her stories were clever and interesting enough to strike the King's fancy and make him care. She wove tales not only to save her own life, but she also saved the King from himself, not to mention the maidens in Persia.

Your brand is unfinished business, an evolving story that needs to be told and sustained over time. If you aren't getting results from using social media, then you need to step back and assess whether you have, all along, been telling a good story. You need to have a whole arsenal of powerfully woven tales blended across multiple platforms: in the press, in articles, in your blogs, in your books, and in your videos, so when you tell your story in bits, tweets, and pictures, your audience will already know who you are. Your audience will already be connected to you. You will have won the hearts and trust of many for *One Thousand and One Nights*.

The P.R. Power of Genuine Story

Remember the Big Kahuna, who chomped cigars and kept his trophy wife in *Christian Louboutin heels*? He thought he had a big story, but the reality is something else was big and it was not his story. Some people think if they hiccup softly, it's news. Understand that your version of what is a story may not really be real news at all. Understand the power of a real story and understand how a real story is different from a non-story or a so-so story.

You ought to think about your audience as being a potential romantic partner instead of a faceless lump of clay that will buy your books, give you a great job, and send business your way. Stop treating your audience as if its only purpose is to serve your needs. Think about what you have to offer your audience. Feel free to be sexy.

Romantic love is one of the most powerful of all human experiences, and there is a lot to be said for perfecting the practice of romancing your audience. If you want to be attractive to your audience, here is some advice for you to think about.

I have observed people promoting themselves in ways that suggest they did not care about romancing their audience. For example, in your Facebook you have at least one Photo Whore. This is the person who documents every moment of her life on her iPhone. It is not enough that she is posting her photos on her own Facebook. She takes it one step further and posts every new photo of herself on your wall and on the walls of all her friends. She is like an old dog peeing the entire perimeter of your front yard just to stake her turf. Rule: Don't post photos or images on your friends' walls unless you know for sure they want them there.

I know of a naturopath who has been doing a video and email campaign by sending emails that have headers in all CAPS saying: Do you have FLATULENCE? Do you have BODY ODOR? Do your FEET SWEAT? She is assuming that the size of her words in all CAPITAL LETTERS is going to generate impact instead of the words she has chosen to convey her message. If people know her, the suggestion that they have flatulence is not a great way to start a "conversation." People who do not know her will assume she is a spammer and hit delete. Rule: Do not use all CAPITAL LETTERS in your emails and especially not in the email subject line or header.

When you are intent on romancing your audience, don't be a failed Comic. The person who is not a comedian and has no comedic talent whatsoever and thinks he's being funny when he's not is just a dork. I saw an accountant who always poses in photos with a large green parrot on his shoulder. I also saw a nutritionist posing with an apple on the top of her head. It just seems goofy. Rule: Don't try to be funny unless you really are funny. If you are going to do things for shock value to get attention, then my advice is to be bad, but sexy like Kim Kardashian. You will also need to have a great ass.

Remember Rod Stewart and his song "Da Ya Think I'm Sexy"? He wore a gold jumpsuit opened in a V-shape to his navel, sporting gold chains and shaggy bleached blond hair.

He received a lot of criticism for that song. Some accused him of betraying his roots in rock and crossing over to become a Pop Disco King.

That song was released as a single in late 1978 and spent one week at the top of the British charts, four weeks at the top of the Billboard Hot 100, topped the charts in Australia, and to date, his video on YouTube has had over 7 million views. Rule: Come hither is better than I will give you everything I've got even if you don't want it.

Do you think I'm sexy? Rod Stewart posed his sexiness as a question, as an opening for a conversation and a romantic interlude. He didn't say I'm sexy and I know it. He sang: If you want my body and you think I'm sexy... just reach out and touch me. He was a tease.

Another example of sexy, but bad, is Lady Gaga. She assumes many personalities, roles, costumes, and she can be shocking, but she never gives you full disclosure of who she is, which is intriguing. There is a sense that even her greatest moments of excess are still restrained, and you know there is more to come. She always holds back. Rule: Be a hussy, not a whore.

Broadway star Patti LuPone is far from classically beautiful. But that voice! Her stage presence is greater than any other actress I have witnessed. When I saw her in *Gypsy*, she stopped the show. I have seen a lot of Broadway shows, but I have never seen a bonafide *showstopper.* The non-stop applause is so thunderous and the standing ovation is such a distraction to the actors that the action on stage just stops. Patti LuPone had the audience begging. After the show was over, the applause would not stop. Just one more song, the audience clamored, but she did not come back. Not that night. Rule: Be a showstopper! Always make them come back for more.

Think of Pope Francis, *the People's Pope*, showing up unannounced in a cafeteria to eat with the working folk. He makes his audience of ordinary people feel special, as if he truly cares about their needs enough to take the time to listen. Who knows where the Pope will show up next?

Dave's Killer Bread is connecting with his audience by saying any of us can make a mistake and go down the wrong path and still turn around to become a good person. Will Dave succeed in his mission to change the world one loaf of bread at a time? Stay tuned.

You don't have to be beautiful to be sexy. You do have to want something and, at the same time, you want to be wanted. You have to offer your audience something that they really want. On both sides, desire hangs in the balance like unspoken electricity crackling in the air. Listen! The most seductive thing you can do is to listen to the person you are trying to seduce. The sexiest conversationalists in the world say little and let others do the talking. Be sexy! Be exceptional! Flirt! Flirt shamelessly, but hold something back. Remember, coyness is a virtue. From there, that is how you will build a lasting romance with your audience. And your audience will extol your virtues for free to the viral masses not because you are so wonderful but because you made them feel wonderful.

6

Getting Away With Murder

Last fall, I got on the Number 6 subway in NYC and sat down next to a *Gangsta* who smiled at me. His jeans were slung low on his hips and he wore a hoodie—that's what led me to believe he was a Gangsta. He showed me the movie on his iPad. "Oh my God, she just killed herself!" he said. He told me he was watching the *Walking Dead* and how the unfortunate woman shot herself with her own gun. My newfound Homeboy (*Homie)* told me all about the horror drama, how it was an ongoing series about a world dominated by flesh-eating zombies and how to tell the humans from the monsters. He told me I just had to get into the *Walking Dead* because I would love it!

As I walked off the subway I assured him I would get into the *Walking Dead* and he seemed kind of pleased that he had won me over. My *Homie* made me think how important it is to tell a good story by showing it and not only writing about it. He inspired me to see the need to include good video storytelling in my P.R. business. I know plenty of professionals who would not step foot in the subway. It's hot down there in the dirty tunnel where people are poor, tired, and dragging around their big bags and backpacks. If I stayed above ground in the town car and rode in a bubble, it seems like I'm protected from harsh reality. But being in a bubble makes us clueless about what is happening in the real world and can cause us to make bad decisions in business and in life.

When I go into the tunnel, I have my ear to the ground. If I didn't ride the subways, I wouldn't even know a Homie from a Gangsta. A Homie is my friend and a Gangsta could kill me. When a Gangsta makes an emotional connection with me he becomes my Homie. In the wrong circumstances any Homie can become a Gangsta. Little known fact: There is no difference between Gangstas and Banksters except rich people don't have to ride subways and Banksters get away with murder.

Being rich will not only buy good P.R. spin and placement in the press, but in some cases being rich can keep you out of jail. Attorneys often use spin the same way P.R. people use spin—to influence juries, the public, and the media. Spin can be used to transform what appears to be a black and white situation into a murky gray area, where there is neither wrong nor right. In the gray zone, someone can be both wrong and right, and there are minute degrees of distinction made between partly right, partly wrong, mostly right, and mostly wrong.

For example, take the Affluenza Defense. The affliction "affluenza," was cited by a psychologist to bolster the legal argument that a North Texas teenager from a wealthy family should not be sent to prison for killing four pedestrians while driving drunk because he had been afflicted by *affluenza*.[14]

Affluenza has been used to describe a condition in which children—generally from richer families—who have a sense of entitlement, are irresponsible, make excuses for poor behavior, and sometimes dabble in drugs and alcohol. The story has been all over the news and I can't understand why more people aren't outraged; but I also have a unique perspective of why we're all so easily influenced by spin. Perhaps most people don't understand that it took considerable money to hire a legal team who would concoct the Affluenza Defense, and even more money was required to hire the expert witnesses. In this case, the psychologists who were paid to assess the situation supported the legal assertion that the Affluenza Defense is a valid psychological excuse to mitigate the seriousness of the crime.

Now consider my poor Homie on the subway who suffers from the misfortune of getting tried for a petty crime in Brooklyn. He does not have the resources available to fabricate a legal strategy as creative as the Affluenza Defense, which is a prime example of the P.R. and legal resources that money can buy. My Homie is going to the slammer on Riker's Island!

Another high-profile legal case using high-wattage P.R. involved the young American woman Amanda Knox, who was convicted along with her boyfriend Raffaele Sollecito of the 2007 murder of Meredith Kercher in Italy. Initially Knox was found guilty in the Italian courts and spent nearly four years in prison before the case was overturned on appeal. The case is full of numerous contradictions, ranging from the actual whereabouts of Knox on the night of the murder to the illegal tampering of the evidence found at the murder scene, as well as the involvement of a third person, Rudy Guede, who was actually convicted of the murder in a separate trial.

Smitten with her beauty, the Italian media painted a picture of Knox as an "angel face" killer. The American press, equally enraptured with Knox's fresh-faced appearance, has frequently asserted her innocence. The murkiness of the facts has made the case the focus of high profile media speculation.

The contradictory views of Amanda Knox that were captured in the press didn't happen by accident. It was widely reported that Dave Marriott, principal of the P.R. firm Gogerty Marriott, dealt with the case on a daily basis while he conceived of many P.R. strategies that helped to counter the negative image of Amanda Knox in the press. By enlisting the support of her friends and family and by gathering their testimonials, he was able to create the perception that this young American woman was casualty of the Italian court system and a victim of the Italian press.[15]

For people who are uninitiated in knowing how P.R. works, it might appear as though friends and acquaintances rose up spontaneously on their own to tell stories that positioned Knox in a favorable light. From behind the scenes, P.R. practitioners often *selectively* interview people to get the necessary testimony that will cast a positive spin on a person or situation. This means they do not interview everyone. They only get testimonials from those individuals who are in alignment with the spin the P.R. practitioner wants to achieve. It is this testimony that is fed to the media, prompting journalists to report favorable news stories about a situation, a company, a politician, or a person.

Creating good spin requires the P.R. practitioner to do three things. First, the messaging platform must be created. The messaging platform is composed of the key messages that you want to send to your target audience. The messages can be quite complex depending on how many target audiences you want to reach. For the sake of simplicity, let's create a key message for Amanda Knox: *She's a beautiful young American girl studying in Italy, and despite her sense of adventure and passion, she is innocent to the harsh realities of the world. While she might be free spirited, naive, and acting with reckless abandon, she is in no way capable of committing a violent crime.* Second, the P.R. practitioner must selectively identify and interview the people who concur in this assessment of Amanda Knox. Third, and most difficult of all, the P.R. practitioner must write up the testimony to craft a compelling story and use it to convince the media of the truth about Amanda Knox.

It sounds easy to find people who will provide testimony that is in alignment with the message you are trying to create. Think again. Developing the art of asking good questions is a dedicated *Machiavellian* pursuit. The P.R. practitioner must be persuasive enough and manipulative enough to lead the witness to say what he wants them to say and in exactly the right tone of voice.

Although Amanda Knox's parents are not wealthy, and may have not had the liquid financial resources to pay for high quality legal and P.R. services to merit concocting a variation of an "Affluenza Defense," the money had to have come from somewhere. In 2012, Knox signed a $4 million dollar book deal and said most of the money went to repay debts incurred for her defense.[16]

Money Does Indeed Buy Paradox

Paradox is the great catchall word—describing phenomenon that cannot be otherwise explained. Philosophers, priests, pundits, teachers, and scientists, even law enforcement use the word frequently. The word paradox is often quoted in the media. This is because the very word itself is paradoxical, i.e., when no one knows what you are talking about, describe it as paradox. Paradox is nothing more and nothing less than—contradiction. Anywhere you find contradiction, you will most likely find paradox.

Paradox is when two competing and seemingly contradictory truths coexist in the same place at the same time. Instead of making a situation appear to be black and white, paradox defines the issues in varying shades of gray. Paradox means a simple explanation for a crime will never suffice. Instead, you are forced to examine the complicated and messy gray areas and live with a resolution that is far from perfect and rarely conclusive. Usually the outcome is found in favor of the party who has the most money. In many cases, the matter remains largely unresolved and simply goes away. Over time, the American public—with its short memory—forgets that a crime has even happened.

The media and the American public have no qualms about coming to terms with paradox. Think of the public as being sort of like cat lovers who accept that domestic cats can be simultaneously feral and then affectionate at a moment's notice. One moment a cat is rubbing against your leg and purring pure adulation and in the next instant the cat can just as easily rob a life. And yet we love them even when we abhor their sadistic cruelty, toying with a small rodent in a complicated maneuver of playful torture that ends when the cat bites off the rodent's head and proudly presents it as a gift.

Try this paradox. There is a story about a young Palestinian suicide bomber who failed in his mission and ended up being tended to by Israeli caregivers, who later found him joking and sharing sentiment with the same *Israelis* he had been trying to kill. The Israelis are people too, he found out, very caring and tending to his wounds. But upon release from the hospital, you can wager he would return to his messianic condition, his homeland in Jenin, and revert to his criminally insane intent— the mission to kill as many Israelis as he could.

There is a mysterious component of the human condition that permits every individual to compartmentalize life in little boxes.

We are disenabled from carrying a complex mixture of emotions with us, and we shelve our dark sides into compartments where they can be hidden away until they burble to the surface and explode with as much impact as a suicide bomber. If only this young Palestinian man could hold his tender thoughts of the Israelis side-by-side with his misguided religious intent to maim and kill. If only he could integrate the contradictory force of his emotions, then maybe he would be able to weep and feel compassion instead of allowing himself to be driven by the compulsion to kill.

Life and business is full of paradox. Americans understand the repulsion of two magnets trying to touch the same pole. Life in a democratic society inevitably invites paradox. America's tendency to be outspoken about many different and competing ideas will always encourage paradox. Democracy by its very nature fosters paradox. Within the context of paradox is the ability to see life's infinite possibilities and at the same time to understand life's sometimes harsh realities. Usually it's only wealth that can buy paradox. Sometimes the poor get a shot at paradox, but it's just dumb luck.

The same paradoxical gray area applies to Amanda Knox. In one testimony given by a family member, Knox is depicted as so gentle that once she cried carrying a spider cupped in her hands to take it outside rather than to hurt it. This innocent and compassionate young woman could not have possibly killed her roommate Meredith Kercher in a delirious sex-game gone wrong.

Michael Skakel is a good example of the accused actually pleading total innocence when it is clear he is guilty of murder. Michael Skakel was accused of killing his neighbor, 15-year-old Martha Moxley. It is worth mentioning that Skakel is the nephew of Ethel Kennedy, widow of Robert F. Kennedy, because it is the Kennedy connection that enabled him to get away with murder.

The Michael Skakel case spanned more than 25 years and inspired worldwide media coverage. Ninety people including Ethel Kennedy, her son Robert F. Kennedy, Jr., and a son of the former Governor Hugh Carey of New York wrote letters to ask the judge for leniency. In the letters, Skakel was described as a very worthy person with a profound sense of humanity and compassion. Skakel had more than two-dozen supporters crammed into the courtroom for his sentencing. Even though the Judge admonished him for failing to accept responsibility for the horrible crime that had been committed, he received a sentence five years short of the maximum penalty that the judge was allowed to impose under state law. Never mind that Skakel's victim Martha Moxley was beaten to death with a golf club outside her home. Twelve years after the murder, Skakel was freed from prison on a $1.2 million bond. Money can buy mitigation for the most heinous crimes.

It is also important to note that the use of paradox as a defense requires the services of skilled lawyers and seasoned P.R. professionals who have good media contacts. Paradox doesn't come without cost. Money can buy loads of paradox. Take Mr. Skakel, who on the night of the crime, just prior to murdering Martha Moxley, had masturbated in a tree while trying to peep into Miss Moxley's bedroom. Yet in the hands of skilled P.R. practitioners the final paradoxical spin positioned Michael Skakel as a nice man who was kind and caring to many people...except for the young woman he allegedly brutally murdered.

In the hands of skilled legal and P.R. practitioners, we come to accept the ambiguity in high profile cases like the ones involving Michael Skakel or Amanda Knox. A good P.R. person will dish up enough testimony and feed it to the press to create paradox, which is composed of contradiction that is intended to create confusion and ambiguity, i.e., gray areas. In the zone of gray areas, no one is completely right, nor is one completely wrong. The world is not conceived in black and white, but in shades of gray. A world painted in gradations of gray allows for people to be deemed slightly right or slightly wrong and every variation in between. When paradox is used as a chief tool underlying spin, the conclusion or legal judgment can arrive at no other outcome than one of establishing reasonable doubt.

You will never be sure about what really happened. After all, a good P.R. practitioner will repeatedly remind you that you were not there when the crime was committed. You may never know the truth about Amanda Knox or Michael Skakel, but in some ways it's beside the point. No matter what outcome you want to achieve, you need to know how to develop your own messaging platform, gather the right testimonials from people whom you know and trust to support your overall P.R. objectives, and convince your audience, especially the media, that your spin is indeed the truth.

Without a wealthy patron paying for P.R. and spin, weaving a paradoxical tale is not possible. If you do not have wealth, there is always the possibility of getting a high-profile influencer to exert the power of paradox for you in the same vein as Émile Zola championing the cause of wrongly convicted Captain Alfred Dreyfus. Someone has to pay for paradox to keep the digital synapses popping. Getting placed in the news doesn't come without a price. Without paradox there are either/or situations: Good guy and bad guy, winner and loser, black and white, with no variations of gray. Among the poor, working class, and middle classes there is an uncanny cultural precedent of presenting complex issues with simple summaries and even simpler conclusions.

Here is my favorite story that is decidedly shocking, but completely devoid of paradox because the perpetrator wasn't wealthy. A crematory operator named Ray Brent Marsh, age 28, had dumped a slew of bodies on his northwest Georgia property instead of cremating them. Ray Brent Marsh took over the operation of the crematory in 1996 after his father who was the crematory owner became ill. Through the years, thirty funeral homes in Georgia, Alabama, and Tennessee had sent bodies to the crematory.

There was no law on the books in the state of Georgia that captured this "crime" of dumping bodies instead of cremating them. Ultimately Ray Brent Marsh was charged with theft by deception for failing to cremate the corpses, one count for each body that had been identified. It took more than 500 people with 43 different government agencies to work on the cleanup. As search teams spent months excavating the grounds of Tri-State Crematory, more bodies turned up, bringing the number of corpses found on the 16-acre property to 331. Many of the bodies were identified by toe tags or by hospital wristbands still on them. Some bodies dated back as long as three years before.

The bodies were disposed with no regard given to the dignity to the dead. Some bodies were stacked ten high inside buildings. Others were left unburied in the woods. One corpse was left in the back of a broken-down hearse. More bodies had been dumped into a lake that drained into a reservoir used for drinking water. It's not likely that Ray Brent Marsh's egregious conduct was motivated by greed. As a matter of fact, Ray Brent Marsh used to charge people a small fee to fish in the lake, but in recent years stopped allowing anyone to fish there. He often yelled at people who entered the property to fish so they wouldn't stray and find the bodies.

A spinmeister never came to rescue Ray Brent Marsh to uncover the reason for what he did. Strange stories about Ray Brent Marsh's true motives began to circulate. Some online newsgroups, web sites, and threads suggested Ray Brent Marsh was a necrophiliac, or worse, into devil worship. And as ludicrous as it might seem, online newsgroups suggested he committed this atrocity due to pure greed. If Ray Brent Marsh was motivated by greed, he could have just burned the bodies in a funeral pyre or disposed of them in a more economical way. The crematory incinerator had broken down and Ray Brent Marsh didn't have the wherewithal to fix it. Without a P.R. machine in place, Ray Brent Marsh was screwed. Until this day, he is still in jail and a move was made to seek the death penalty.

Hard evidence during pre-trial hearings suggested that Ray Brent Marsh loved his family, was never considered a threat to the community, and was unlikely to commit additional felonies. A good spinmeister would have delved into his I.Q. and school records to uncover that the boy was a tad short of a brick. Don't ever mistake someone for being evil when they're just dumb. A clever spinmeister can make the devil seem fun, entertaining, and very human.

If you have money and a good story, you can get away with murder. The saga of O.J. Simpson, his butchered blonde wife Nicole, and her friend Ronald Goldman had people glued to the TV for weeks. Americans love drama. Soap operas, HBO movies, Movies-of-the-Week, and Reality TV command a huge market share of viewers. Fiction or non-fiction, Americans want to hear a good yarn. They love a good story well told. If you can spin a tale with strong characterization, a fair plot and the elements of sex, fame, murder, betrayal, and money, you will achieve a large audience. In America, you can be as bad as you want and still get away with murder. You don't even have to feign innocence or seek ways to mitigate the brutality of the crime.

Once you've committed murder, an element of plausible deniability can be artfully woven into the scenario. This is when the very rich are able to hire a high-powered defense team to plant doubt within the minds of reasonable people—the jurors. Plausible deniability always includes the fine art of spin. Those who weave spin, lawyers, P.R. professionals, endeavor to create an altered reality—unbelievable, but true.

In the case of O.J. Simpson, his preposterous claim of total innocence worked. O.J. was acquitted of the criminal charges. One important thing to remember about O.J. Simpson is he was already a highly sought after and popular public figure. He also had money—lots of money. If O.J. Simpson had been your average poor white guy in Tupelo, Mississippi, with a decimated pension fund, a high mortgage, and no job, he would be on death row. Even though O.J. Simpson maintained his total innocence and beat the criminal rap, he was still held accountable in his civil suit. The innocent plea can work, but you have to possess enough money. Mounting a defense for the rich takes on a different set of rules and there are different consequences in the end. And even with loads of money, sometimes paradox doesn't get the perpetrator completely exonerated for his crime.

Still, in the final analysis, O.J. Simpson never went to jail for murdering two people.

Murder isn't only about killing people; there can also be financial murder. Take the situation with *Enron*. The energy trading giant's collapse became—for a time or at least until *WorldCom*—the biggest bankruptcy case in US history. At the pinnacle of the Enron scandal, Kenneth Lay, ex-Enron CEO, suddenly retreated to the background. Instead his blonde trophy wife Linda Lay took center stage. In a strange twist of spin, Kenneth Lay had nothing to say. Linda Lay went to bat for her husband, *Kenny Boy*, and proclaimed his total innocence. In January 2002, Linda Lay appeared in an interview on NBC's *Today Show*. Linda Lay said: "Nobody even knows what the truth is yet. The only thing I know, 100 percent for sure, is that my husband is an honest, decent, moral human being who would do absolutely nothing wrong. That I know 100 percent."

The wife of ex-Enron CEO Kenneth Lay said her family lost its fortune when the energy trading giant collapsed and her husband had done "absolutely nothing wrong" in one of the biggest bankruptcy cases in US history. Linda Lay defended her husband as a decent and moral person who was fighting hard against personal bankruptcy. "Other than the home we live in, everything is for sale," she said. "We are fighting for liquidity. We don't want to go bankrupt."[17]

Linda Lay was asked what had happened to the reported $300 million in compensation and stocks her husband earned over the past four years. Linda Lay said the couple relied on now-worthless Enron stock and had never diversified their portfolio. "It's gone," she said. "There's nothing left. Everything we had mostly was in the one stock." Then she added they were also under pressure due to cash calls on their long-term investments. Then she went on and made a pitch for her husband's innocence. She used the classic strategy of *switch the blame* and the wrongdoer suddenly became the victim. Linda Lay said her husband, who quit as chairman and CEO of Enron, had been grossly misunderstood by the public and media, and was the victim of "mass hysteria."

Linda Lay said she could understand the anger and loss felt by Enron employees about her husband's upbeat statements encouraging employees and the public to buy more stock just before the company dived. Much of the criticism of Ken Lay centered on evidence that he knew of the energy company's debt-ridden position even as he was advising people to buy Enron stock, which was worthless. Linda Lay said, "If I were back there listening to all the things that were being said I would absolutely have to say, 'What is wrong here? How can all of this be happening without someone doing something terribly wrong?'" She said there were many things her husband had not been told that would come out in the many investigations now under way. "Those things will all come to light and that's what we're all praying for." Someone was else was to blame. Kenny Boy was just another victim.

On camera and on cue, Linda Lay broke down and cried while she recalled a couple of days before Enron collapsed when her husband came home from work and said he could not turn the company around. "He said he had tried everything he could think of and he could not stop it," she sobbed, adding: "[He was] devastated, devastated for his employees." Asked how she felt toward those who said her husband had betrayed them, she replied, "We've lost everything, but I don't feel Ken has betrayed me. I'm sad, I'm desperately sad, but I don't know where to place the anger. I don't know who to get mad at. I just know my husband did not have an involvement."

The Enron saga took a tragic and more sinister turn with the apparent suicide of J. Clifford Baxter, who had resigned as vice chairman of Enron Corp in 2001, and who was said to have opposed the accounting practices of the company. Linda Lay said her family was devastated by Baxter's death, adding that her husband had spoken to him not too long before his death. "Cliff was a wonderful man. It's a perfect example of how the media can play such havoc and destruction in people's lives. This is the ultimate. This is a loss of life. It makes my heart, it makes Ken's heart ache." She added, "Had we known, we would have picked up the phone and called him. We would have gone and been with him. We would have done anything we could to have helped him, helped his family, but we had no idea he was in that kind of pain."

What unwitting Americans didn't know is the high powered and very expensive P.R. firm Hill & Knowlton taught Linda Lay how to cry on TV. P.R. professionals from Hill & Knowlton carefully scripted Linda Lay's performance, tears and all. When the Enron story broke, Kenneth Lay's sister, Sharon Lay, placed a distress call with M.A. Shute, an executive with Hill & Knowlton. The P.R. firm had represented Enron in the past. When Sharon Lay called, M.A. Shute was vacationing on a yacht in the Caribbean. "Get back here right now," Sharon Lay demanded. "We need your help!"[18]

Hill & Knowlton is highly skilled in the fine art of spin. Corporate damage control is their specialty. Quick background check: Hill & Knowlton has transformed the leaders of Latin American death squads into agents of compassion and mercy, tobacco companies into health advocates, and toxic waste generators into environmental crusaders. Of course, Kenneth Lay could not talk and defend himself. His lawyers had advised him that anything he said would be used against him in court. So he sent his wife forward to be his advocate of spin. Hill & Knowlton's M.A. Shute moved into Sharon Lay's Houston home and spent a furious week coaching Linda Lay and the rest of the Lay family members on how to present themselves to the media. Then it was off to NBC's *The Today Show*.

After the accelerated coaching session, Linda Lay presented herself as distraught and grieving, a lonely housewife whose membership in the local Houston country clubs might be endangered due to the tragic downturn in her husband's finances. Her husband *Kenny Boy,* according to Linda Lay, was as much a victim as the lowliest Enron shareholder whose pension had dissolved into thin air. He had done no wrong. Instead, the wrong had been done to him. Evil advisors had sabotaged his company. "He didn't know what was going on," she said. Now the Lays face poverty and deserve compassion, not jail time. "We're broke," Linda moaned. "We're selling everything we own." Even as the tears streamed down Linda Lay's face, the Lays reportedly still owned over a dozen properties valued at more than $10 million in the Houston area. None of them were on the market. There was also a $14 million vacation home in Aspen, Colorado.

In America, getting away with murder always takes into account the tool of *Plausible Deniability*. As long as you can assert a measure of reasonable doubt, you are on your way to being exonerated of all wrongdoing. The key is to always blame someone else for your own transgression. The blame placed on someone else must always be reasonable, *plausible*. Take the plight of Linda Lay. It was plausible that *Kenny Boy* really didn't know everything that was going on his company. It was plausible that the media really did find him guilty without giving him his day in court. And finally, it was plausible that there was a tribe of evil wrongdoers (other Enron executives) who sabotaged the company.

Clever P.R. spinmeisters will create so many gray areas that you will no longer hold Kenneth Lay accountable simply because he was in charge. Forget the operative principle that he is the CEO and he had a fiduciary obligation to be responsible no matter what had happened.

When you are highly skilled in the fine art of spin, you can create an altered reality. Weave a tale that captures America's heart. One caveat: all the facts have to add up. Linda Lay had fatal flaws in her argument. The evidence was undeniable. *Kenny Boy* did know of the Enron's financial dilemma when he issued the edict to buy more stock. And the Lays did take a big financial loss, but they didn't stand to lose it all. The true victims of Enron are ordinary people who invested money in the company.

BP Oil's Leadership and Its P.R. Strategy

Enron's Linda Lay may have put on an Academy Award-winning performance to exonerate her husband of all wrongdoing, but the leadership of BP Oil during the Gulf oil spill failed to get away with murder. BP Oil must ask itself if it could have saved tons of money if it had credible and sincere leadership in place instead of Tony Hayward, who was clearly ill-prepared and ill-suited to do the job. Instead of projecting the integrity and the commitment to solve a problem, Tony Hayward came off as *Mr. Fancy Pants*, a petulant British schoolboy who pretended to be attacked by a bully when he indeed had taken the first swipe at something as small as sweet as a baby sea turtle.

In all of his stammering, sniveling and dropping of selfish little bon mots, the question remains: Was Tony Hayward ill advised by his swarm of P.R. advisors? It is doubtful that Tony Hayward could have gotten so much bad advice, not with the millions of dollars being spent to prop him up and to make him look good before the cameras of a global audience. It is entirely plausible that the innate material itself was seriously flawed—even with the best P.R. coaching in the world, Tony Hayward just wasn't good enough to rise to an occasion that called for serious leadership.

Despite the failure of BP's leadership, its P.R. strategy was so effective that everyone including the staunchest environmentalists referred to the disaster as an oil spill instead of naming it for the catastrophe that it really was—an outright volcanic gusher of oil. When you think about it, a spill comes from a barrel or a ship and it can be contained, but a gushing leak from the ocean's floor demands a different type of raison d'être and response altogether. So BP's P.R. machinery has done a good job; here we are, all of us calling this disaster a spill as if it was the smallest of environmental mishaps, a tiny oil hiccup, a little brown bubble washing out to sea.

Getting Away With Murder Means There is Nothing Left to Lose

A discussion of people who get away with murder would not be complete without mentioning the iconic Mel Gibson, so eloquently featured in the film *Braveheart*, to whom the concept of *freedom* apparently means the ability to bash Gays, Jews, and Women with equal hatefulness. Even Mel Gibson seems to have a hard time being Mel Gibson. He has a long history of angry and violent outbursts, coupled with numerous bouts of public drunkenness. Still, no matter how heinous his back trail, he is worth a billion dollars and, whenever he chooses to do so, he can fuel a change in how he is perceived. If an oil volcano can be perceived as a spill, then Mel Gibson stands just as great a chance of turning around his brand. Maybe he will go into rehab and start a foundation that rescues Gulf wildlife from the oil so long as he doesn't have an anger problem with dolphins.

For most of us, we are professionals and entrepreneurs who do not have luxury to afford to screw up like Mel Gibson. We are working professionals, and we may be accountants, lawyers, medical doctors, chefs, educators, designers, scientists, or IT specialists, and we really don't have the time or money to get caught up in a juicy scandal. We can afford to finance our lifestyles, our business ventures, our families, and our savings & retirement, but we do not have the money to finance strategic P.R. operations that can undo any damage that is done to our professional brands. P.R. can be expensive, and the most expensive form of P.R. of all is crisis management and damage control.

So if you don't have the money or expertise to fix your broken or sullied reputation, you really do not have the luxury of screwing up.

Do everything in your power to prevent your pants from falling down in the first place. You can't afford to make the type of high profile mistakes made by Tiger Woods or Mel Gibson. So don't be stupid. Don't ever assume no one is watching or no one is listening. Today, everyone has a camera embedded in their cell phones and a craven desire to take anyone down a notch in order to experience *Schadenfreude*, which loosely translated from German is pleasure derived from the misfortune of others. Schadenfreude may be a private feeling, but then there is *Open Schadenfreude*, which is outright public derision. In the new media world, pleasure derived from the misfortunes of others has become more than a very popular mass movement; *Open Schadenfreude* is the new zeitgeist. We just love to make people roll around in the detritus of their own greed, corruption, lust, and misguided carnality, but only if they have been caught in the act. We want them to pay the price, not so much for what they did, but for getting caught!

Not all of us are stupid and we don't screw up on purpose. More often than not, we are only human, and humans make mistakes. Some are honest mistakes and some are not. And then in other instances, stuff just happens in the normal course of this messy business called *life*: a high-profile divorce where the bickering goes public, a custody battle over minor children, a bad parting of ways in a job, a relationship, or with a business partner. The unwanted trouble in your life could be an illness or a death or loss of the family business. Could be alcoholism, drug dependencies, or a debilitating illness you don't want anyone to know about. Maybe your child is responsible for a crime or has driven while drunk and gotten into a car wreck. Could be domestic violence or an angry feud among siblings over the distribution of assets in their parents' estates. Could be getting stalked by an unwanted lover or even a psycho. Sometimes it can be an out-and-scandal—a hand caught in the till, or a tawdry sex affair. You could be beset by murder—a murdered spouse, friend, or business associate. Every day things happen to us, good or bad, right or wrong, that are out of our control and pose a danger to our reputation. Bottom line: everyone needs to learn how to get away with murder.

Managing one person's brand is a more precarious task than it is to manage the brand of a company. If something goes wrong with your own professional brand, you can't fire your management team. And more often than not, you do not have the resources to hire legions of P.R. teams to do damage control for you.

Always keep in mind that you, the entrepreneur, cannot do P.R. like a company or a mega-rich celebrity, but you might be able to implement a beautifully orchestrated damage control if you have, all along, maintained a strong brand and you get the right advice from a trusted P.R. advisor. You can't conduct crisis communications or damage control solely as a *Do It Yourself*

P.R. campaign, and you ought to seek expert P.R. counsel. In fact *Do It Yourself* P.R. is the equivalent of pulling a tooth that has already abscessed. It's time to let the experts get to the roots to contain the infection and cut it out.

One of the finest examples of the enactment of the art of American spin belongs to the New York P.R. professional Lizzie Grubman. In July 2001, Lizzie Grubman backed her father's Mercedes SUV into a crowd outside the Conscience Point Inn, a Southampton nightclub. During the final moments before the crash, when nightclub bouncers tried to get Ms. Grubman to remove her car from a fire lane, she addressed them with expletives and called them white trash. She then proceeded to crash her SUV into an unwitting crowd of onlookers and injured 16 people.[19]

Ms. Grubman responded by admitting the wrongdoing and took full responsibility for her actions. She pled guilty to the felony charge of leaving the scene of an accident and a misdemeanor assault charge. And most important of all, she apologized. Ms. Grubman then mounted a strategic offense that was honorable, proactive and full of symbolic remorse. Looking gaunt and puffy-eyed in court, she claimed the whole ordeal caused her to lose weight to 95 pounds and below size zero. She was accompanied to the courthouse by a thrall of glamorous supporters who wore black and arrived in long procession of dark colored SUVs, an image that connoted both the importance of her persona, but also her unquestionable remorse.

In her letter to the judge, Ms. Grubman stated she had engaged in "soul searching" since the crash. She explained the circumstances in a calm, rational manner, which included all of the juicy details. The morning before the crash, she had learned that her mother needed immediate surgery for ovarian cancer. She went to the Hamptons only because a client had insisted she attend a restaurant opening. At the last minute, the client canceled the event. In her own words: "I sent home the driver that was supposed to take me and my employees to the restaurant opening, figuring that I was not going anywhere that evening. It had truly been the worst day of my life." She ended up at a clambake, then the Conscience Point Inn, where she said she had planned to drop off friends and stay briefly. "My stay at the Conscience Point Inn did turn out to be brief," she stated. "But I will remember it forever."

In a well-publicized interview with *New York Post* gossip columnist Cindy Adams on October 21, 2002, Lizzie Grubman told why it would never happen again.[20] She sat in Cindy Adams' home for two hours and didn't eat, drink, or smoke. Mostly, she cried, and repeated over and over: "I'm scared. I'm so scared." And: "I'm stupid. I'm so stupid." "Please, I'm not looking for sympathy. I was stupid to leave the scene of an accident. I can't explain...but I was, like, in shock. Everyone taking over... hollering, telling me what to do... pulling me away, pushing me out of there. I had no control over anything. It was panic."

She went on to describe how it would never happen again because she recognized the enormity of her crime and chastised herself openly. "People were injured. Nobody should ever, ever, ever leave the scene of an accident. I think about that every day. I don't know how I did it. It was a crisis zone. People thought they were doing right... I'm so sorry. I want to hit myself in the head. There's no excuse. I deserve doing the time. I deserve punishment for leaving the scene."

In her efforts to make restitution, Lizzie Grubman explained: "I pray for those who were hurt and beg their forgiveness. I can't send them a note. Can't send flowers. Can't hold their hands. Can't contact any of them. I want to say so much, but my lawyers won't let me. I can't even explain to you now what I want to. I can't... until... this is all over." Amid many tears Lizzie Grubman proclaimed the full extent of her restitution: "I pray people will understand... please... I'm not a horrible person. This terrible experience portrays me as an animal. I'm not. Please... there isn't one waking moment I don't think of those who were hurt."

P.R. professional Lizzie Grubman gave a brilliant rendition of what to do when one has committed murder, or at least when one has attempted murder. She admitted the crime; she explained the circumstances, and most important of all, she apologized. She made her apology credible by explaining why it would never happen again and what she would do to make restitution. Then she willingly and contritely accepted her sentence to spend 60 days in the Suffolk County Jail as part of her plea agreement. She was also sentenced to five years of probation and 280 hours of community service. After her sentencing, she was handcuffed and taken to jail. Jail officials stated Grubman would not get special treatment behind bars. But like any other inmate with a similar sentence, with good behavior, Ms. Grubman could be released in 40 days. Ultimately, Ms. Grubman was released in 38 days over the Thanksgiving holiday and returned to work—as usual—the following Monday. Having fessed-up in full, Lizzie Grubman got away with murder.

Although Lizzie Grubman played out a superb strategy of crisis communications and damage control, one that saved her own life and kept her from doing long-term jail time, keep in mind three important factors. First, she came from wealth (she's the daughter of entertainment lawyer Allen Grubman. In 2001, *Newsweek* called him "perhaps the music industry's wealthiest and most powerful attorney".). Second, as a P.R. professional, Lizzie Grubman knew how to successfully stage a P.R. campaign and manipulate the media. Third, she already had a relationship with powerful journalists who would buy into her spin and tell her side of the story. All of these factors together illustrate how unless you are a savvy P.R. practitioner, you should not conduct damage control as a *Do It Yourself* P.R. campaign; you ought to seek expert P.R. counsel.

Getting away with murder is not easy. Now I speak of *murder* metaphorically. The murder might be some sort of egregious conduct (a sin) or the murder may be an actual murder. Either way, getting away with murder, real murder or metaphorical murder, is not guaranteed. There is a challenge. The challenge is how much money you will be able to throw at your case. There are no convicted murderers sitting on death row who are wealthy. Aside from being convicted of murder, the inmates on death row only share one other attribute in common. Across the board, death row inmates are unequivocally poor. With no dollars or legions of P.R. professionals and well connected attorneys spinning paradox to judges, juries, the public, and the media, the poor rarely get away with murder. It is important to keep in mind that murder is only one form of evil. There are many others.

7

Evil Comes in Many Shades of Gray

Years ago, I was having dinner with a well-known British literary author. He had not shaved and as usual he was wearing a baseball cap indoors to hide his thinning hair. He ordered the most expensive wine on the menu, a 1998 Penfolds Shiraz Kalimna Bin 28. (He knew I was picking up the tab.) During our conversations, we had an ongoing dialogue, a clash really, that was somewhat sophomoric, about good and evil, to sin or not to sin. How can we understand *Mysterium Iniquitatis,* the mystery of evil in the world? Are all people both good and evil? He mentioned, "Some of my closest, dearest friends who personally knew Mother Teresa said that at times she could be just a ghastly beast." "Is gossip a sin?" I asked. He looked at me and grinned. "Sin can be anything you want it to be," he said.

Whether you believe the devil exists or not, doesn't matter. What matters is that you can look at P.R. the same way you can look at the devil. According to the British author C.S. Lewis, "Some people take the devil far too seriously and other people do not take the devil seriously enough." Same holds true for P.R. Some people take P.R. far too seriously. Some people do not take P.R. seriously enough.

Many P.R. professionals will share their tips to get media coverage, and I am no exception, but here is the harsh reality of the situation. Sometimes you don't need to have any media contacts at all to place a good story, but you do need to have good media contacts when you really don't have a story, and you're just making something up, which is more often the case than not.

I know the CEO of a high-tech P.R. firm, who stated in a room full of people that the only reason she got her client feature coverage in the *Wall Street Journal* was because she was a big blonde from Texas who had large breasts.

Everyone knows there is a dark side to P.R., but we really don't talk about it. No one really wants to believe that what you are reading in this morning's *New York Times* has been placed by a cunning P.R. person who is being paid lots of money to leverage her relationships with key journalists. We want to believe that most journalists are ethical and they are looking at a potential story to determine if it is timely, relevant, and compelling enough to put their bylines and their reputations on the line. We don't want to believe that a story is being shaped by the size of the P.R. person's breasts or what connection is made between P.R. people and journalists after hours in a bar.

Take the public unraveling of the life of *New York Times* technology reviewer and self-proclaimed gadget guru David Pogue. His romance with Silicon Valley P.R. executive Nicki Dugan sent tremors the size of an earthquake through the media world. At the time Nicki Dugan worked at the San Francisco P.R. firm OutCast Agency representing tech companies such as Amazon, Facebook, Cisco, Netflix, and Yahoo. During the time when they were involved, Pogue had written numerous articles about OutCast clients and their competitors. Not only did Pogue fail to cite a potential conflict of interest, but he also had a wife who might have taken umbrage at Nicki Dugan's announcement of her romance with her husband on Dugan's Facebook page. Pogue and his wife have since divorced after a heated domestic scuffle involving the police that had his wife alleging the gadget guru hit her in the head with an iPhone. The story made the front page in local Connecticut newspapers.[21]

Romance has created conflict of interest since the beginning of time. Still, most people underestimate the power influential P.R. people have on journalists and the stories that they tell. Another media earthquake slammed Silicon Valley when it was revealed that Facebook had secretly hired P.R. firm Burson-Marsteller to pitch anti-Google stories to the press alleging Google was invading people's privacy. The rivalry between Google and Facebook is all about who will dominate online advertising.

Facebook's plot against Google backfired when a blogger turned down the P.R. firm's offer and squealed. The story about the whistle blowing blogger, the deceitful P.R. firm Burson-Marsteller, and its whisper campaign on behalf of an unnamed client (Facebook) broke in *USA Today*, and ironically, not in the purported transparent world of social media. Social media gurus will have you believing that the conversation on social media is all about transparency and how traditional P.R. spin is dead, but they are not taking account that the devil is very real, has metaphorically large breasts, and is doing a superb job feeding stories to the press. Word of warning to journalists: If you do encounter the devil, don't stare too long. She might see it as an opportunity to pitch you.

What is Sin and Should We Care?

A frank discussion of evil would not be complete unless sin is examined. To sin or not to sin? Good question. To sin or not to sin is also a paradox. Think about the following statement. It's a *test* really: Sin is the destruction of ourselves as well as the destruction of our relationships with others. According to my friend, the British literary author, "If it's inherently destructive and causes harm to one's self or others, then it's sin."

Everyone knows the Judaic-Christian litany of sins: envy, wrath, gluttony, lust, pride, sloth, and greed. Mahatma Gandhi, one of the most influential figures in modern social and political activism, had something to say about sin. Gandhi viewed sin as being off the mark or out of spiritual balance. Gandhi, too, had seven deadly sins. He considered seven traits to be the most spiritually dangerous to humanity. Gandhi's Seven Deadly Sins are: *Wealth without Work, Pleasure without Conscience, Science without Humanity, Knowledge without Character, Politics without Principle, Commerce without Morality, Worship without Sacrifice.*

No one knows why sin exists. No one really knows why evil exists. The tales and parables derived from every belief system under the sun, from Greek mythology to the Koran, cannot adequately define *Mysterium iniquitatis*, the mystery of evil in the world. In the end they all fall short because they rely on mythology—fiction, metaphors, and archetypes—to explain what really cannot be explained. The origins of evil have not been defined as an absolute truth. No one can agree or attest to the empirical validity of any religious discipline. Adam and Eve eating an apple from the tree of knowledge is a great story but it just isn't plausible as an explanation for *Mysterium iniquitatis*, nor is the image of Lucifer falling in disgrace away from God's love and plummeting into an inferno named hell.

I am not a shrink or a therapist and I lack academic credentials in psychology. However, as a P.R. professional, in a peculiar sort of way, I'm expert at understanding how evil comes in many shades of gray, and I feel eminently qualified to talk about sin. I have observed plenty of evil at the behest of people who are willing to pay any price to attain wealth and fame.

While we have discussed sin in all its glorious detail by referencing the traditional Judaic-Christian seven deadly sins and Gandhi's Seven Deadly Sins, there are specific American sins that ought to be explored. These are the sins that are antithetical to achieving the P.R. goals that are explored in *American Spin*.

Everyone Lies, But Not Everyone is a Liar

In America, one rule we abide by is that it is wrong to lie. However, the underlying reality is everyone lies, but it is not okay to be a liar. Now as long as I remain relatively neutral on the subject, I intend on telling you the truth. This is no small feat. P.R. professionals, by their very nature, are good liars, not great liars. The realm of great lying is reserved for other choice professions: lawyers, doctors, police officers, accountants, politicos, any public official, drug dealers, Hollywood producers, filmmakers, reality TV stars and talk show hosts, fools and beggars, Presidents of the United States, Kings, consulate heads, the diplomatic corps, and consorts. No one is exempt from lying.

People lie because telling the truth will cost them. The loss they will suffer may be great or it may be small. Status, power, love, respect, and money are some of the big losses or the potential gains. People are always afraid of losing something. People always want something and have their own hidden agendas. Most lies are told as a matter of convenience. When it's too much trouble to take the time to explain the truth, a lie is easily sprung. *Great liars lie to gain money, power and to cover their routine transgressions—their sins.*

There is no truth that satisfactorily explains why lying is a sin. Maybe no one describes lying as a sin because everyone does it. Sooner or later everyone lies. To be human is to lie. The question is how often do you lie? Have you made a career out of lying? Do you lie when there is no clear and compelling reason to lie? If you lie for no reason, then you can be branded as a liar and that is an unpardonable American sin.

Now here is the trick. Spin must contain an element of truth. Spin is not outright lying, but a method of artfully packaging the truth. Once you put it out there for public scrutiny, there are too many variables and too many people who can unravel your spin and expose the lies that you cleverly tried to conceal. If your spin is unraveled, then it can damage your brand, no matter if you are a person, a product, or a company.

Sometimes Lying is the Right Thing to Do

In America, it's okay to lie when the person had no business asking a particular question in the first place. Once when I was interviewing for a job as a director of P.R. for a technology company, I lied to the Big Kahuna. The Big Kahuna was aggressive, high-powered, and fancied himself as being as smart as a whip. His interview covered many personal questions, some I was willing to answer truthfully and some I was not. Given the line of questioning I began to form some opinions about my interviewer. It was clear to me that he did not mind working with women so long as they weren't encumbered by other interests, such as a life outside of the office. (Anyone in the working world who has half a brain knows employers secretly discriminate against women with children because of all the sick leave they imagine they will take, leaving their single counterparts toiling until the wee hours of the morning.)

Twice during the first part of the interview, the Big Kahuna asked me if I had children. "Do you have any children?" He grinned like a friendly old woman who really liked children, had a couple himself, and wanted to swap photos of our kids. Both times I lied and said no. The third time, he said out-of-the-blue, "Any children?" I looked him in the eye and said: "None that I am aware of."

Of course I knew his question was illegal, the guy was a jerk, and I could have turned him into some regulatory agency, but I did want the job. So I lied. I got the job. I was good at my job. (I never called in sick, unlike my single counterparts who were frequently late for work due to habitual carousing, and bouts of drunkenness because they had no one to go home to.) With all due credit to the Big Kahuna, he didn't get mad at me when he found out I did have three children. Nor did he try to retaliate. He simply said: "Amazing."

There are nice lies. A nice lie is when you compliment your friend's ghastly haircut because there isn't anything she can do about it but wait for her hair to grow back. There are white lies. A white lie is when you dodge the question and don't tell your cousin she looks fat when she really does know she is fat, otherwise she wouldn't be asking the question. Then there are boldfaced lies. The boldfaced lie is when you don't tell your wife you were out with another woman, and refer to your "date" as John.

There is the one lie that has always been held sacrosanct— *the holy lie.* A holy lie is told to protect life. A holy lie is not mysterious. A holy lie is blatant and powerful. The Nazis come to your front door and ask you if you if you have seen any Jews. (Three Jewish children are hiding out in your basement.) You tell the Nazis, "No." A holy lie is that simple. You can't rationalize or spin a holy lie. To borrow the Latin phrase, *res ipsa loquitar*, the thing speaks for itself. A holy lie is a sin of perfect goodness.

The power of a single lie is enormous. A lie takes on a life of its own because it often takes innumerable small lies to cover the trail of the first one. Always remember it may be worth your effort to take the time to tell the truth, the whole truth, and nothing but the truth. Consider weaving spin by strategically layering the facts in a way that stages what should be revealed now and what should be revealed later.

If you want to lie effectively, you will need to have an excellent memory. Paradoxically speaking, although everyone lies, no one enjoys being lied to. Everyone aspires to some semblance of the truth, albeit even if it is his or her own version of truth. And despite the human propensity to lie, no one wants to be branded as a liar. Consider your persona, who you are and the message you are spinning to the world. Is your word good? Can your loved ones count on you to tell them the truth? Are you able to look yourself in the mirror without wincing? And if you are lying habitually and not wincing, then you are a total sociopath and even the best spin will not save you unless you pay legions of spinmeisters lots of money.

To Thine Own Self Be True

One cardinal rule that cannot be bent or broken: No matter what, don't ever lie to yourself. Lie to yourself and you are on the verge of losing your soul. Remember the ultimate goal of P.R. is to have a good life. You can't have a good life if you lie to yourself. Always know where the bodies are buried so you can walk around them.

P.R. Truth and P.R. Lies

P.R. professionals have the talent, skills, and experience to craft great stories. P.R. professionals are paid well for this expertise. It is a major faux pas to lie to them. Tell the truth. You need to give your P.R. firm all of the correct information so they can be effective on your behalf. Withholding vital information is the equivalent of going to a doctor to get a diagnosis when you have withheld disclosing half of the symptoms or what you believe to be the true cause of your illness. If you don't trust your P.R. firm to keep confidentiality, then there is a simple solution. Have the firm sign a non-disclosure agreement. But tell the truth. If all the cards are not out on the table, no one can plan and execute an effective P.R. campaign.

As a P.R. person, I have been called upon to lie. During the dot.com crash when I was working with the Big Kahuna, I spent my last month there working without a salary. So did the rest of the staff. The management team kept promising to pay, but they couldn't come up with the money and as a result everyone was laid off. The word hit the streets. Around the clock, I was getting frantic calls from media and the company's investors—at work and at home even though I was technically no longer employed by the company.

The Big Kahuna called me into his office, which housed a 100-gallon aquarium of tropical fish, an unused Stairmaster, and a broken Foosball machine. The Kahuna was red in the face, almost crimson, and—looking extremely haggard despite his recent face-lift—told me not to respond to the media. Not responding to media is a cardinal sin in the P.R. world and I told him so. Then he asked me to lie, to say everything was okay, funding was right around the corner. I stared into his Aquarium and saw little dead bodies of brightly colored neon fish floating to the surface. The water level had gone down. I was thoroughly insulted. Not only did he want me to lie, he wanted me to lie without getting paid to do so. Against his wishes, I did respond to media by issuing a statement that the *company had suspended operation until further notice*. The moral of this story is a P.R. person should never put her reputation on the line and lie to the media.

In Flagrante Delicto

In *flagrante delicto* usually means getting caught in the midst of illicit sexual activity. Examples of professional brands mired in sexual sin include the public marital infidelities of Al Gore and John Edwards. Again, these men are more than business professionals or entrepreneurs; they are high profile public figures who have spectacular financial resources available to do damage control. Keep in mind that if your egregious misconduct is one love affair, it is a lot easier to do damage control. Ultimately, the world admires and forgives people who give up their worldly status, fortunes, and political ambitions because they have finally found one true love. The whole world loves a lover. Even David Pogue's scandalous affair with Nicki Dugan seemingly had a happy ending when he proposed marriage to her in a slick video that ultimately went viral.[22]

The American people tolerate most sins of the flesh. John F. Kennedy and Bill Clinton's sexual antics in the White House became the fodder for late night entertainers and talk show hosts, more than they became reasons to destroy their public images. If anything, the notion of Bill Clinton asserting *"I did not have sex with that woman"* (Monica Lewinsky) boosted sales in cigars. The image of Bill and his cigar inspired lampoon cartoons all over the Internet and especially in *Cigar Aficionado Magazine*.

Eliot Spitzer, on the other hand, had a rough go and still has yet to turn around his fall from grace. His stint with the *Parker Spitzer*, the one-hour show on CNN that he co-hosted with political columnist Kathleen Parker, was not a good "I'm sorry" vehicle to make anyone forget or minimize Mr. Spitzer's wrongdoing. The fact that he would pair himself with an attractive woman and occasionally engage in fake on-the-air flirtation is the wrong way to repair his brand image. To compound matters further, behind-the-scenes reports indicated there was actually non-stop bickering and fighting going on between Spitzer and Parker. Trying to re-invent himself as a political commentator who flirts with his partner on-the-air but bickers with her behind the scenes is too similar to the real life situation he may indeed have had in reality with his wife, who ultimately left him. The on-the-air bickering served as a constant reminder of what he did wrong.

Everyone would forgive his folly fully if the show had decent ratings, but the *Parker Spitzer* show was consistently plagued with low ratings. No matter what Mr. Spitzer has done wrong, Americans love a great comeback. To turn around his brand, Mr. Spitzer should have been seen doing "good works" everywhere, with his wife perpetually on his arm, smiling glowingly for every photo op at every high profile charity event. He could be the next great goodwill ambassador to the world. The Spitzers could have appeared on the talk shows together sharing their feelings publicly—talking about the pressures of public life and the toll it took on their marriage. It was the constant stress and pressure that contributed to his need to find an outlet, to become more "human" in a private and dark place where he no longer had to play a public role.

If Mr. and Mrs. Spitzer had played out how his crisis had rejuvenated their marriage and love for one another, in every major media outlet (broadcast TV, radio, online interviews, traditional press, and social media) for at least a year, then he had a chance of moving on with his life and staging a real brand turnaround. The major obstacle, as I see it, is Mr. Spitzer did not seem to know how to apologize well. And he does not know how to keep his apology alive. Humility does not seem to come naturally to him, and he has not learned yet how to embrace it, or for that matter, fake it on-the-air or in person. Eliot Spitzer can still turn around his fall from grace, but to do so he must find a new Mrs. Spitzer. By all recent accounts, his wife Silda has left him.

Do You Think No One is Listening?

In America it is a sin to be naïve by behaving as though no one is listening when you are indeed being heard by someone. Your brand reputation is only as good as your messaging. People forget that everything they say or do is a message. And sometimes messaging isn't only what you say but it is how you treat other people, including the people whom you think of as dismissively as though they don't count. For example, I am aware of a CEO candidate who didn't get the job because of what he tweeted on Twitter. His tweets were not unethical, illegal, immoral, or untoward in any way. His tweets just showed lack of judgment and exhibited poor leadership skills.

Twitter has become increasingly important as a tool to use to interact with the media. Many people do not consider that if they are using Twitter their tweets are a form of messaging. As a result, their tweets are indiscriminate, careless, and sometimes downright sinful.

Who could forget former New York Congressman Anthony Weiner tweeting salacious messages and photos of his privies to women he met online? Lust, pure and simple, and it brought him down. His last name *Weiner* is now an even more popular way to describe the appendage that he was showing off. Lust is easy to spot. It's sort of how Supreme Court Justice Potter Stewart defined the test for obscenity as "I know it when I see it." Twitter lust usually means photo sharing: breasts and bulging crotch shots. Naked or not, your brand message is clear.

Most sins are not nearly as graphic as lust, but they have ramifications. Take Gluttony. Are you using herding services to falsely inflate your following? No one will know exactly how you got so fat with followers. Like Falstaff, who is a great archetype for all fat, happy-go-lucky, yes-men & suck-ups, you're just popular and flirty, the life of the party, and everyone wants to be around you. No one questions whether you're a fabulous foodie who has easy access to popular celebrity chef eateries or you pigged out daily on boxes of double-stuff oreos and MacDonald's french fries. Being fat with herded cows doesn't explain why you have so many followers. Everyone knows you're a loser who can't control your appetite.

Greed is easy to spot and it doesn't look good. Most people are NOT tweeting their fees and salary requirements. Although I have seen professionals who do have compliance and legal requirements totally forget the rules and tweet: "Call 1-800 for a free consultation today!" You can spot the greedy because everything they tweet, news articles, blogs, quotes and quips, has to do with money. Most people have the sense to not try to sell products on Twitter, and yet authors, who are the greediest and most desperate of all, are always giving discounts on their books that no one will read, even for free.

Twitter Envy is boasting how you are bigger and better. The Envious Tweeter has knee jerk responses to every major event. He is the one who tweets "FIRST!" as if he is Christopher

Columbus who intentionally arrived in a strange and foreign land without ever admitting he was off course and made a wrong turn. He is the thief who tweets other people's newsfeeds as his own without giving due credit or a proper retweet (RT).

Twitter Anger walks into the bar looking for a fight. Send him a direct message, you will be flamed. If he sends you a direct message, he tells you someone is saying bad things about you on the Internet. Or he'll threaten to send you a picture of you NAKED through a cam. The angry tweeter spends too much time looking for a rumble. Twitter is the Wild West and on every corner there is a cheap saloon and an opportunity for a big brawl.

The Twitter account that spews out 12 tweets in a row from Hootsuite is from Sloth. Sloth doesn't have an original thought and doesn't want to think because it is too much work. He reposts, retweets, and knows how to copy and paste a slew of inspirational quotes from quotations.com. Sloth doesn't have the energy to build a following and can easily lapse into Gluttony and buy followers, but he has been so lazy for so long that he doesn't have any money.

Pride knows Twitter is a great tool to build his brand and to gather intelligence about what others are doing, so he takes the time to develop a targeted audience. Pride spends no more than 15 minutes a day on social media because he has a strategy. Pride knows spewing random, mindless thoughts and quotes by famous people is sort of like pissing in the wind. He will not tweet a lewd photo because he knows that no one could have a bigger appendage than he has. Like Ashton Kutcher, Pride wants 17 million followers and he will do anything to get them, even if he has to buy them or steal them. But he will not beg. And he will make it appear as though his legion of followers came on their own. Pride is envious of anyone whose tweets eclipse his own, but he is a strategic thinker and will not show anger in public. Pride creates false accounts and starts rumors, both good and bad, on Twitter. Of all sins, Pride is the only one worth pursuing. It is the only sin that works.

Pride is the ultimate sin of the devil. Remember what brought down Lucifer? He wanted to be God. Pride is much more than being the ultimate narcissist. Pride is Machiavelli and he wants total control. It's always all about me, but I'll fool people into pretending that it's really about them. Pride is the sin of the consummate P.R. professional, and it works extremely well.

I am not here to make moral assessments as to what is right and wrong or to establish the baseline for some of life's most complicated ethical issues. Morality, religion, ethics can all be used as tools by savvy P.R. professionals to manipulate hearts, minds, and purse strings. I do not want to get complex enough to discuss what is right or wrong, or situational ethics such as what is right in one situation and what is not in another. Realistically though, we are all human, and we do make mistakes. Unless you are a sociopath, in your private moments you must know in your heart of the times that you have screwed up. And even if you are truly a sociopath, as many successful people are, you do not want to be perceived as one. Generally, it's not good for business to be thought of as a sociopath.

No matter how unpardonable or unspeakably morally reprehensible and obscene some American Sins seem to be, they can all be forgiven. Any sin can be diminished, and over time it will dim in the public memory. Truth be told: Each day, we are inundated with so much information and digital debris, that we forget most events, even scandal. From Bill Clinton's antics in the White House to the pedophile priests in the Catholic Church, *lust* permeates every aspect of our culture. Lust is more than about sex. Lust is also an unquenchable desire for power. Lust for power can be far more seductive and durable than sex or even love. There are no laws against *gluttony*, but life isn't easy for the 27 percent of the American population who are morbidly obese. Being fat is not against the law, but it does make getting a job difficult, climbing the corporate ladder improbable, and becoming a star or attaining leadership status challenging. On the other hand, maybe some fat Americans aren't gluttons at all but are full of sloth and fail to exercise. Both anger and envy lead to the formation of criminal intent and result in many forms of violence. Sin is never simple.

The Whistleblower as Evil Incarnate

There is only one American sin that can never be forgiven and that is when someone steps forward to tell the truth. A whistleblower is a person who tells the truth about corruption in a government, a company, or an organization in a way that challenges the status quo. One whistleblower is former US civil servant Linda Tripp who was the integral player in the Monica Lewinsky scandal that led to the impeachment of US President Bill Clinton. Tripp secretly wiretapped her phone conversations with Monica Lewinsky that recounted Lewinsky's affair with Bill Clinton. Linda Tripp paid a price for her whistleblowing. She was lambasted by the press and at the close of the Clinton administration, she was fired from her job at the Pentagon.

Another person who was fired for telling the truth is Carmen M. Segarra, the bank examiner who had worked with the Federal Reserve Bank of New York.[23] Ms. Segarra was among a group of bank examiners that found Goldman Sachs had inadequate procedures to prevent conflicts of interest. This practice had previously resulted in a disastrous outcome for Goldman Sachs' clients during the financial collapse of 2008. New guidelines were meant to stop Goldman Sachs from putting their pursuit of profit ahead of their clients' best interests. Ms. Segarra found that Goldman Sachs was not in compliance with the new guidelines and refused to change her findings even after she was asked to do so by top management. Two weeks later she was fired.

Another case in point is the Challenger space shuttle catastrophe. Roger Boisjoly was an American mechanical engineer, fluid dynamicist, and an aerodynamicist who had raised objections to the launch of the Space Shuttle Challenger before the spacecraft exploded. Roger Boisjoly had warned about problems with the O-rings and advised his managers on numerous occasions that if the problem was not fixed, there was a strong probability that a shuttle mission would end in disaster.

No action was ever taken. Instead Boisjoly was shunned by his co-workers and he was forced to resign. Who could forget the ill-fated day in January, 1986, when seven astronauts, including a schoolteacher, were killed when the shuttle exploded 73 seconds after liftoff from Cape Canaveral, Florida?

The vilification of the person who upholds the truth is not native to American culture. The whistleblower archetype has been long-branded as having a Promethean quality. In history, individuals who had a penchant for Promethean forethinking have suffered and been persecuted. Sailors who foresaw the possibility of disaster and warned their shipmates to steer away from danger have been executed for insubordination. Although Prometheus is the Greek mythological equivalent of a *David* going up against *Goliath*, he was often deemed to be a lowly challenger to the omnipotent power of Zeus.

Prometheus means *forethought,* which is a thinking process most often attributed to true intellectuals. Intellectual thinking leads to an analysis of breaking apart and dissecting the components of a custom or system in order to improve on the old way of doing things. Essentially, Promethean thinking is the bedrock of innovation. And while innovation is often revered in the American culture, especially when it makes money, there is also great resistance to change, especially when the old guard stands to lose money, power, or prestige. It's no surprise that in the mythic sense, Prometheus has often been associated with being the snake in the Garden of Eden. Prometheus, like the whistleblower, gets people to open their eyes and to eat the fruit of knowledge and in doing so disrupts the order of nothing short of God.

The whistleblower is the ultimate entrepreneur, a lone maverick, going up against the status quo or a cultural norm. And while the whistleblower has the courage to speak up about injustice, corruption, or what is flawed and dangerous in a given system, he or she is never knighted or nominated for sainthood. If anything, the whistleblower is a gadfly, a nuisance, a disruptive force in the universe who should be dealt with severely and silenced. In *Self-Reliance*, Emerson said, "For nonconformity, the world whips you with its displeasure."

As a cultural phenomenon, the only way to have the privilege of whistleblowing and telling the truth—without fear of retribution—is if we cloak it in humor. As touched upon earlier, the truth can only be told, without fear of retaliation or retribution, under the guise of being funny, by popular comic entertainers like Jon Stewart and Stephen Colbert. In American culture, the biggest evil of all is to tell the truth when the *people-in-charge* do not want to hear the truth. The wagons will circle and you will be ostracized, vilified, thrown under the bus, and left for dead. There is no pardon and no way back to the fold. Telling the truth upsets the status quo and calls into question the power of the people who are on top.

8

The Rich Will Always Flee to the Top

I grew up in Yonkers as a working class kid and learned the NYC subway system on my own. When I was 13, I played hooky from school and rode the IRT, now renamed the #1 train. I rode the subways during a time when muggings were commonplace and gangs ruled New York City's underground. Although I no longer live in New York, when I return on business, I still ride the subways. I never know what I might see or who I might meet. There is one thing for certain that I've learned from taking subways on my own at a young age: I will always know how to find my way to the top.

Most people are not aware of what it takes to get on the cover of *The New York Times Magazine*. People at the top know how to get great press. It is one of the benefits of having enough money to hire a *spinmeister*.

For example, recently there have been a wave of stories about Lee Radziwill in the media,[24] especially in *The New York Times*. Radziwill, now in her eighties, is known as a socialite and younger sister of the former first lady Jacqueline Kennedy Onassis. You might remember Radziwill's failed attempt at an acting career in the 1960s or you might recall her associations with high-profile husbands, friends, and lovers. You might not remember any of these things, but when you think about it, there is little difference between Lee Radziwill and Paris Hilton or Kim Kardashian, all of whom have made careers out of being famous.

In the spring issue of the February 7, 2013, *New York Times Magazine*, Lee Radziwill was strategically positioned as a woman "who proved that she can still be super-sexy at 79." Sidebar comments from famous people include Hollywood it-girl of the moment Sofia Coppola. The article stated, "In a world of passing celebrity, Lee Radziwill, 79, possesses a timeless aura that radiates nowness."

The story of Radziwill's spectacular *nowness* was further amplified in a NYT video that was made by Sofia Coppola.

Although Coppola was off-camera during the interview, you could hear the little-girl-in-awe tone in her voice as she asked Radziwill questions. On camera, Radziwill recalls going on tour with the Rolling Stones and Truman Capote, a splendid summer spent with Peter Beard at Andy Warhol's house in Montauk, N.Y., and a childhood so lonely she tried to adopt an orphan.

Then in an ironic twist of P.R. spin, in the May 30 *New York Times Magazine*, Sofia Coppola gets her own separate news story. This article strategically positions Sofia Coppola as the essence of *nowness* who really does not want to talk to the media because it is such a bother to have to give up her privacy.[25]

Coppola's interviewer turns out to be, of all people, Lee Radziwill, and every time Radziwill asks Coppola a question, she first frames the questions by talking in great detail about herself. Together, the two women revel in their *nowness,* their coolness, how much they admire one another, and most important of all, how both women fiercely protect their privacy and disdain media attention.

Wow! How much does *nowness* cost? You might think Lee Radziwill is in so many *New York Times* cover stories simply because she's fabulous. This kind of P.R. is not free and is, in fact, very expensive because it's not really news; it's *nowness.* You might wonder if Lee Radziwill and Sofia Coppola share the same P.R. firm. At one point, when Radziwill is interviewing Coppola, she talks about the fact that "Everybody wants to be out there until you're so sick of their faces and their magazine covers that you think, 'Oh no, not again.'"

Every time we see Lee Radziwill or Sofia Coppola, we can say the same thing: "Oh no, not again." It's not that they're bad people. It's just that there so many more people who are truly accomplished and deserve recognition. There are many people who have done amazing things who are not getting in *The New York Times* because they can't afford the high price of fame.

Bernard-Henri Lévy: The People's Pig

The self-proclaimed French public intellectual Bernard-Henry Lévy, who was born into great wealth, once reportedly said, "I knew when I was 20 that I'd never have to suck up to anyone."

He often associates himself with other notable men, such as Charles Baudelaire, André Malraux and T.E. Lawrence. Anointing himself the successor to Alexis de Tocqueville, Bernard-Henry Lévy toured America as if it were a freak show. The result became his book *American Vertigo*,[26] where he spends a great deal of time interviewing drag queens and lap dancers as if they are the bedrock of American culture. As always, Lévy is known for being short on the facts, long on bombastic puffery.

Being wealthy and a self-proclaimed public intellectual is a big cross to bear for someone who might just be an average guy. While Lévy fancies himself an erudite thinker in the same vein as Victor Hugo or Émile Zola, his tireless social antics make him cheap fodder for the gossip columnists on both sides of the Atlantic. He once boasted that his sexual prowess makes him take as many partners as possible in one night. He'd attend a dinner party with one woman only to end up in bed with another woman that evening, and by morning he'd visit the bed of still another woman. You know what they say about a man who brags about his sexual escapades? It usually means something is quite small, but it's probably not his ego.

In an attempt at being iconic, Lévy brands himself with his initials of BHL and claims to be known everywhere far beyond his native country of France. He frequently compares himself as charismatic as Jesus Christ and sports crisp, white shirts and an immaculately groomed gray mane that is clear evidence of a legion of on-call stylists, makeup artists and wardrobe professionals.

There is a French term that quite succinctly captures this sort of person: *poseur*. And money can buy a whole lot of pontification, preening and punditry, also known as *publicité*.

Lévy's most important works are often described as inaccurate and sophomoric. Take his book *Who Killed Daniel Pearl?*,[27] based on the *Wall Street Journal* reporter who was captured in Pakistan and murdered in 2002 by Islamic extremists. In a moment of sheer disrespect, Lévy wrote a fictionalized version of what Daniel Pearl was thinking just moments before he was beheaded. One can hardly imagine the perils and horror of Lévy's war coverage trying to get to the bottom of *Who Killed Daniel Pearl?* Did he ride embedded with the troops in Afghanistan, or did he travel far above the hoi polloi with French President Jacques Chirac's special envoy? It is important to note that one benefit of Lévy's wealth has meant that he has never bothered to learn how to drive and is frequently chauffeured around Paris in a Daimler sedan.

Everyone is entitled to their quirks, and Lévy is no exception. While it's true he was born into great wealth that is not a reason to lambast him. What is unforgiveable is his passionate defense of his friend, Dominique Strauss-Kahn, former managing director of the International Monetary Fund (IMF), after Strauss-Kahn's physical assault on a hotel employee, Nafissatou Diallo, in 2011. Lévy proclaimed he couldn't believe that a simple chambermaid would have the audacity to step forward and make a formal complaint against such an important man.

"And what I know even more is that the Strauss-Kahn I know, who has been my friend for 20 years and who will remain my friend, bears no resemblance to this monster, this caveman, this insatiable and malevolent beast now being described nearly everywhere," Lévy stated at the time. "Charming, seductive, yes, certainly; a friend to women and, first of all, to his own woman, naturally, but this brutal and violent individual, this wild animal, this primate, obviously no, it's absurd."[28]

A recent search for Bernard-Henri Lévy on the *New York Times* site reveals 672 results, as the subject of feature articles, or the source of quotes, references and other mentions—and this is only in the *Times*. Lévy has not done anything substantial enough to get so much ink in top-tier legacy press.

His social media also boasts big numbers. To date, he has 19,367 likes on Facebook and 12,000 followers on Twitter, but we all know anyone can buy social currency. It can only be a matter of money stoking the P.R. machinery to buy *publicité* on both sides of the Atlantic. So Bernard-Henri Lévy, indeed, will never have to suck up to anyone.

Having money will keep you out of the news too. Take the untimely death of Keith McCaw, baron of the cellular empire led by his brother Craig McCaw. In 2002, Keith McCaw died in a hot tub in his Lake Washington home. He was only 49 years old. At the time of his death, during fiscal year 2002, he was listed as the 232nd richest American and his net worth was believed to be $970 million in holdings. Not only was he rich in his own right, but the source of his wealth was founded upon old money. The circumstances of McCaw's death remain shrouded in mystery. For reasons unknown, the media never pressed for the potentially prurient details. So while money will buy plenty of press placement, it will also keep a tight lid on the truth and protect the privacy of the rich, no matter what the circumstances are, even a mysterious death.

When Woody Allen's adopted daughter Dylan Farrow described how she was sexually abused as a seven-year-old, a media stampede came to his defense. Dylan Farrow claimed Woody Allen committed a sexual assault that included "inappropriate touching." Legions of bloggers and journalists—aspiring to achieve success in Hollywood—reported the story as if they had been there with Dylan Farrow and were eyewitnesses who could vouch beyond a reasonable doubt that Woody Allen was innocent of all wrongdoing.[29] Woody Allen's vocal supporters ranged from Actress Scarlett Johansson to film producer Harvey Weinstein. Weinstein, by the way, had come to Roman Polanski's defense years earlier and had declared that Polanski's underage rape victim, Samantha Geimer, looked 31 years old, not 13.

What plays out as news in the media is often a clash among P.R. titans. The P.R. firms who represent Woody Allen, Roman Polanski, or Harvey Weinstein are expert at creating the gray areas, the story angles that douse the flames of scandal, and getting these stories placed as news. In the media, if you want to put out a fire, create a gray area.

People of great wealth use spin to manipulate how the media reports the rise and fall of markets: stocks, bonds, metals, commodities, real estate, even art. For example, art has become a commodity and not a cheap one. Decades of easy money and unbridled greed have created an art world where only a very few at the top get to decide the price of an artist's work. There are so many artists who are shut out and will never get a chance to get a fair wage. Today's explosion in art prices, $150 million for Picasso's *The Dream* or $80 million for Jasper John's *False Start*, seems obscenely excessive. The art world has become a playground for hedge fund investors and powerfully wealthy speculators. I expect to see the development of an equities market for art full of unregulated financial instruments with tranches, credit derivatives, short sells, and credit default swaps. At least when this market crashes, no one will lose their homes. I hope.

The essence of art is a visual conversation between the artist— the world inside of him and the world around him. It doesn't matter so much what the viewer of art thinks or feels. Art, unlike P.R., isn't created solely to connect with one's audience. Art is sort of a standalone medium. Sure you can have an artist tell you that he wanted to create a message, and talk to you, but at what cost to his art? He doesn't really need to talk to you at all to make his art. An artist who dwells on the needs of his audience will only find disappointment. An audience does not really know what it thinks or what it feels because they are a group of lemmings that can swim one way or just as easily swim away in another direction. Art is a gift and it matters not what price is paid to declare its intrinsic worth. Yet the stories of art traded as high-priced commodities among mega wealthy men are reported in the press as though it is hard news.

The question remains to be asked: Who pitched this story to the press and what was in it for them? Every time a new story appears about Picasso or some other dead artist in the press, ask yourself why. Someone has paid P.R. professionals to wage a new awareness campaign for these dead artists because it bolsters the high price of their art and the net worth of the collectors who own the art.

Whether spin is told as a news story or through visual media such as print ads, online ads, or videos, the source of the spin must be scrutinized. When Sheryl Sandberg was promoting her book *Lean In*, she took out full-page ads in *The New York Times*. Similarly, Aerin Lauder's launch of a new fragrance line garnered full-page ads in *The New York Times*. This is not to suggest the intrinsic quality of a book or a fragrance; it simply means Sandberg and Lauder have the money to promote their products in the most expensive media outlets that command mindshare today. The ads were placed in *The New York Times* at the same time while soft news stories appeared as all points bulletins in every facet of traditional press as well as social media. More than ever, it is critical for people to understand how much money is needed to buy the spin-making machine that gets glossy feature coverage in top-tier press.

According to data from the Council of Public Relations Firms, there are an estimated 600,000 to 800,000 P.R. professionals in the United States. Futurworkplace, Inc. estimated the number of US public relations practitioners to be closer to one million.[30]

More often than not, it takes significant capital to afford the retention of a P.R. firm, and especially to retain the services of a firm over an extended period of time. The high price of P.R. places it in a luxury category. And as a luxury only the wealthy can afford to pay for the services provided by a P.R. firm.

Two professors of economics, Emmanuel Saez and Thomas Piketty, have spent over a decade tracking the incomes of the wealthy, the poor, and the middle class in countries all over the world. Their work has shown that there is a widening gap between the extremely wealthy and the poor and the middle class, and they suggest that this inequality is comparable to the wealth disparity that existed just prior to the Great Depression.[31]

With the widening gap between the mega wealthy and everyone else, it is logical to conclude that much of the soft news that is reported in the media is placed there by people who can afford to pay the high price of P.R. There is no hard data to support this contention, but it is plausible that it is the wealthy among us— corporations, organizations, families, and individuals—who are paying for the services of an estimated 800,000 professional P.R. practitioners. If it is the rich who are paying for the legions of P.R. consultants and P.R. firms, then it can be unequivocally stated that the media has become increasingly the playground of the rich.

That's not to suggest that people who are less than wealthy can't do their own P.R. They can launch their own P.R. initiatives. It's just that loads of money can buy so much more press attention and a higher quality of placement across all media platforms. It can also be asserted that the public tends to embrace spin when there is so much splashed everywhere through the range of media platforms from TV, cable, and radio to top-tier press, community papers, industry trade magazines, online media, blogs, and all forms of social media, from YouTube and LinkedIn to Facebook, Instagram and Twitter.

Money buys more press; and money buys a higher profile in top-tier legacy media. Legacy press is primarily considered to be the mature newspaper and television news outlets that believe they are the ultimate media authority on any topic. Not only do the legacy news organizations fail to acknowledge what P.R. entity is behind their news sources, but they often omit important information and tend to report a story by emphasizing some aspects more than other, and that is clearly spin. With this understanding, everyone who reads, sees, hears, or observes media must take into consideration how much money it took to buy visibility in the press and identify the source who initially pitched the story to the press.

Hard or Soft News?

Everyone can get into *The New York Times* if she commits a heinous crime, gets involved in a high-profile sex scandal, or dies in a plane crash, but that's hard news. Soft news requires a different approach. Soft news is found in the lifestyle, business, and arts sections of any newspaper. The definition of soft news is it's both informative and entertaining. The dissemination of super sexy soft news is the chief function of the Sunday *New York Times Magazine*. Behind every great soft story in *The New York Times*, you will find a spinmeister.

Spinmeisters have been around forever. Edward Bernays, the founding father of Public Relations, said, "In almost every act of our daily lives, whether in the sphere of politics or business, in our social conduct or our ethical thinking, we are dominated by the relatively small number of persons—a trifling fraction of our hundred and twenty million—who understand the mental processes and social patterns of the masses. It is they who pull the wires which control the public mind, who harness old social forces and contrive new ways to bind and guide the world."

It is amazing that Bernays stated this commentary in his landmark treatise *Propaganda*. The reality of spin and propaganda is the same now as it was in 1928 when Bernays wrote his book. The only thing that has intensified is the manifold increase in the volume of information that has accelerated through self-publishing, citizen journalism, online media, the blogosphere, and social media.

Returning to the concept of hard and soft news, it is important to keep in mind that even hard news has soft news components. Consider what happens when a hard news story begins trending and many spin-off stories start playing out across media and social platforms. Take the case of Air Malaysia 370 that disappeared mid-flight March 8, 2014. Speculation ran the gamut to include stories of stolen passports, suicidal pilots, crazed hijackers, terrorist groups, continual false reports of wreckage, and mysterious pings vibrating through the Indian Ocean only able to be measured by satellites orbiting the earth. Add to the mix mounting tension between the Chinese and Malaysian authorities with a sprinkling of Iranians seeking asylum in Europe, and you have an international debacle.

We may never know what happened to the plane. If I were Boeing, the manufacturer who built the plane, I would much prefer an aura of intrigue playing out in the press than speculation about the mechanical and electrical integrity of the plane. The possibility of the plane's structural failure would mean Boeing could be liable for a lot of money. This is not to suggest that the Boeing P.R. people had planted a few pitches to help stir the speculative tide and muddy the waters. The message here is to scrutinize everything you read, see, and hear in the media. Whether stories are pitched or planted, there is never a way for the public to know the source *behind* how news stories really originate and how much money is involved and the actual size of a P.R. budget for a particular campaign.

Speaking at a reception marking the launch of the New England Center for Investigative Reporting at BU, Seymour Hersh, a Pulitzer Prize-winning journalist and an author, spoke about the current state of investigative reporting. "Newspapers across the nation are in serious trouble, pummeled by the recession, by declining revenue and readership, and by competition from round-the-clock online resources."[32]

With the decline of legacy media, having the resources available to fund investigative journalism has mightily diminished. Instead what has taken its place is widespread proliferation of native advertising and sponsored content, also called branded content. Native advertising might have many definitions, but it is content that does not appear to be advertising per se and is intentionally made to appear indistinguishable from organic content, i.e., genuine news stories. This type of media placement has always been known among P.R. professionals as *pay for play*.[33]

In the last year I have had some remarkably good story pitches about experts, issues and trends that were steered away from the editorial side of the magazine. Instead editors suggested, "This is a great story as sponsored content. Our journalists will write a 300 word article and include three original photos for $5,000."

In defense of the new *pay for play* news placement, editors and producers assert that native advertising and sponsored content fits better with their editorial content, adapts better to mobile platforms, looks better on a tablet or smart phone, and streamlines the chaos of competing brands vying for content placement. The reality is that extolling the virtues of the new *pay for play* is the media industry's own version of spin. And it's true. What editors and producers assert about the rise of sponsored content and native advertising is true. But like all good spin, it's not the whole truth. Bottom line, native advertising and sponsored content is a rich revenue stream for media outlets to replace the traditional advertising revenue that has dramatically declined. Many media outlets intentionally create *pay for play* content to appear to be very similar to genuine news stories. The power to place a news story, native advertising or sponsored content, is now firmly in the hands of only those who can afford to pay to play.

The Power of Money

Let's return to a most important topic—Money. Money and the lack thereof—it's a moral conundrum that has been with us since the beginning of time. In America, there are many ways to be considered among the top. The many ways to rise to the top are related to all different types of money: working class money (lotto winners), upper-middle-class money (derived from professional services and working as the equivalent of a doctor, dentist, or lawyer), European money (can be aristocratic money), Arab money (oil money that isn't in Texas), sheltered money (could be Asian money), laundered money (from pizza parlors and gambling operations), drug money (and other illicit forms of revenue), dirty money (from porn), celebrity money (based on luck, timing, and talent), mafia money, old money, technology money (companies derived from being in the right company at the right time, e.g. Microsoft), hedge fund money, and luck-of-the draw money (also derived from being in the right place at the right time)... just to name a few.

Money. Everyone wants it. Not just anyone can have it. Not just anyone gets it. Money is the ultimate American aphrodisiac.

The subject of money will get your rapt attention quicker than sex, food, love, or any other human craving. Acquiring money is an essential, but flawed, American value. Americans have a paradoxical relationship with money. We love money and we hate money. Americans believe the right to pursue money is as inalienable as life, liberty, and justice for all.

Many Americans spend many waking hours and even more sleepless nights worrying about money. We work hard to earn money. We scheme of ways to make easy money. We believe we have a chance of winning the lottery. In droves, we actually buy lotto tickets. We dream of how we will spend money as soon as we get it. We can never have enough money. And we do terrible things to be able to hold onto our own money or to take someone else's money.

In America, we have been led to believe that its acquisition is an equal opportunity pursuit. Americans revere wealth with a messianic fervor that approaches religion. After the decline of the Roman Catholic Church and the slow but steady decline of all organized religions, money may indeed be the new religion. American culture measures its very definition of success by money.

Americans may be the most materialistic human beings on the planet. When author and philosopher Ayn Rand wore a $$ sign around her neck, no one laughed. No one paid much mind to the $$ sign icons hung from Ayn Rand's neck or fastened broach-like to her chest. Where else in the world would you see an author like Ayn Rand be taken seriously? Ayn Rand was fond of wearing dollar $$ sign medallions around her neck like some sort of tribute to a pagan god. And the god of Ayn Rand was indeed capitalism. American money.

Americans are imbued with a collective cultural obsession with money and are trained from the time they are infants to know money counts. They also know there is no more important measure of value in American culture than money. The American way of life has surpassed all traditional values and left them by the wayside to wither away in gorgeous platitudes best stated by politicians. Through the artful use of spin, we have been trained to believe that if we achieve wealth, we will have a better life.

Money is more than a tool. Money, and having lots of it, is the only true path to instant gratification. Americans don't seem to feel alive and show excitement unless they can buy frequently and *Buy Now*. The ability to buy vast quantities of consumer goods at a slightly discounted price is what drives the shopping madness of Black Friday, where hordes of consumers camp out in lines to be among the first to enter a store. Black Friday hysteria is so entrenched in our culture that people have been trampled and have lost their lives in order to gain access to the holiday bargain bonanza.

The money amassed by one's endeavors measures success in jobs and careers and even hobbies. Money may be the only true yardstick used to measure affluence, comfort, security, and peace of mind. Americans are so obsessed with money that the amount of money you possess may be society's only true measure of your human worth, your life, and even your death. It goes without saying that the more money you have, the more you can buy P.R. and can use paradox to your own benefit. And as we have already established, with money you can even get away with murder. Rich men have never sat on death row and rich boys and girls don't serve on the front lines of war. From getting away with murder to defending the honor of this country, the people who reign on top are never required to put their lives on the line.

Some types of money may appear to be better than other types. The quality and longevity of a person's money is directly related only to the sophistication of his network. It is your network that will help you not only to succeed in life, but to stay on top... and also, when necessary, it can give you the ability to flee to the top. You can't do anything you want unless you have enough money, and even then there are the network issues, meaning which social and business circles are you permitted to join? Although it seems people of old money have no problem mingling with people who have newly obtained wealth. Witness the rise of celebrities keeping company with old money or with Wall Street money.

Having money means being able to buy anything, even intangible things like power, prestige, and fame, without ever having to pay the true price—if you have enough money, you'll never have to go into debt. If you have enough money, people will even respect you and grant you small favors for no other reason than the commanding nature of your money.

The trip to the top could have been achieved strictly on one's own merits or the person could have been wired in because he was born on third base. It doesn't matter how people arrive at the top. What does matter is when people who are at the top only stay there and associate with others at the top, they tend to develop a disconnect from reality. And yet it is the people who have been moneyed-up and who are living in an insular world inside of a bubble at the top that are making decisions for everyone else.

There was a wonderful article written by *New York Times* columnist Paul Krugman that suggested that the rich are invisible.[34] Krugman's discourse on the invisible rich began with a brilliant juxtaposition of a past socio-economic analysis of the *Invisible Poor*. In his article Krugman stated, "Half a century ago, a classic essay in *The New Yorker* titled 'Our Invisible Poor' took on the then-prevalent myth that America was an affluent society with only a few 'pockets of poverty.' For many, the facts about poverty came as a revelation, and Dwight Macdonald's article arguably did more than any other piece of advocacy to prepare the ground for Lyndon Johnson's War on Poverty."

Now Krugman is asserting that the American public does not have a clear understanding of how much the rich own and control because the rich are so far removed from the hoi polloi. While I admire Krugman, his thinking, and his work, if you examine the rich within the context of what gets reported as ews, the rich are not invisible at all and dominate the media with startling transparency. Do the reverse engineering on any story in the business press and identify the source. You will quickly understand who has power, who has money and who controls most of the media and news that is communicated to the American public.

Individuals and businesses who do not have wealth or the resources to fund aggressive P.R. campaigns are at a disadvantage and unable to break through the clutter. Having money means being able to buy anything, especially the P.R., to ensure that all things intangible like power, prestige, and fame are wrapped into the stories that are told to the press.

The irony of life among the rich, however, is not nearly transparent enough for my taste or for you to understand that money may be important, but not everything. Remember that spin—that realm belonging to the artful manipulation of P.R. professionals everywhere—makes the rich appear to be truly enviable, even when their lives may be as miserable and as tragic as your worst nightmare. The rich will always flee to the top, but it doesn't mean they get out alive. Nobody does.

Being rich, notwithstanding the human things that happen to everyone, makes it easier to get a quality education, to start a business, and to get wired in to the best social and business networks that money can buy. Being rich makes it easier to be an entrepreneur and to grow a successful business. The superrich can pay for the P.R. that will get the powerful press attention to increase awareness for the business in order to help it grow. One way everyone can achieve some semblance of economic parity and opportunity is by being powerful observers of what is being reported in the media and learning how to use this information to his or her own advantage. It also means people need to observe who is fleeing to the top and how they are getting there. There is no better case in point than Rose Freedman, who followed the rich to the top and saved her own life.

Until recently, Rose Freedman was the last living survivor of the Triangle Shirtwaist Fire. Rose Freedman was a young Jewish woman who worked for a sweatshop in New York's garment district during the early 1900s. Young women, mostly immigrants, some of whom barely spoke English, worked long grueling hours for pitifully low pay. There weren't any labor laws in effect to offer them protection. The young women were treated terribly; some were abused outright, beaten, humiliated, docked sixteen-hour-day-wages for purportedly minor infractions—such as the *I don't like the look on your face this morning* kind of infraction. Like anyone, they had to eat, but their choices consisted of a few hard crusts of bread, thin porridge, gruel, or a potato. The women were young, poor, uneducated, and hungry. There was nowhere else for these young women to go. Rose Freedman was one of those young women.

As the end of the workday approached on Saturday afternoon, March 25, 1911, a horrendous fire broke out on the top floors of the Asch Building in the Triangle Shirtwaist Company. Within minutes the entire building became engulfed in flames and smoke. There was pandemonium and an attempt made at mass exodus as the young women frantically tried to get out of the building.

The executive team saw the ensuing madness and terror and worried about the material costs, the losses due to potential theft. They made a decision to lock down the building so the young women would not take a few bobbins, thread, or fabric on their way out the door. (The fact that cloth could never rid itself of smoke damage had no bearing on their decision.) This was an executive decision, a way for the rich to keep down the poor, to keep them in their place, and to hold onto a few extra bobbins, mere pennies. And that is the power of greed when it manifests itself in purely paranoid thinking. In reality, good girls don't steal even under duress. The lockdown didn't save anyone money, it only prevented young women from getting out of a burning building alive.

Within minutes, the quiet afternoon erupted into madness, a terrifying moment in time, disrupting forever the lives of young women who could not find a way out. Outside the Asch building, on the streets below, people passing by witnessed the desperate leaps of the young women from the ninth floor. Having witnessed the smash of bodies hitting the ground, the city of New York would never be the same. The aftermath of the Triangle

Shirtwaist Fire at the beginning of the 20th century had the same impact and political underpinnings similar to the destruction of the Twin Towers on 9/11 that took place almost a century later. By the time the Triangle fire was over, 146 of the 500 employees had died. Most of them were very young women—the immediate co-workers and friends of Rose Freedman.

Rose Freedman separated from the crowd and saved her own life. She saw what was happening, kept her cool, and thought logically about how to get out. She survived the fire by running up one flight of stairs, to the top floor. That's where the company executives worked, and she figured they would have a way to escape. She was right. Rather than unlocking any of the doors below to save the women, the executives had fled to the roof, where they were rescued.

Rose Freedman's harrowing experience speaks to two elements important to *American Spin*. First, a person must know when to separate from the group and trust her own instincts. Rose Freedman didn't succumb to the collective hysteria of her own group—other young women factory workers banging up against a locked door—and saved her life. The second gem of wisdom has to do with knowing when to align yourself with the right group. Rose Freedman knew which group stood the best chance for survival. The moral of this story could be to keep your eye on the rich and watch where they go. But it has more to do with knowing when to be a master of self-reliance and trust your own instincts as an individual. Choosing the right group is a secondary consideration. No group might have the best chance of survival and you could end up alone. Being smart and alone is preferable to being a great, but dead, team player.

The survivors of the Triangle Shirtwaist Fire were left to live and relive those desperate last moments. Rose Freedman was one of those survivors, but she found a place for her agony. True grit, courage, and determination were the chief hallmarks of her personality. She lived on and became an outspoken voice in the political movement to support reform in US labor laws. As a middle-aged woman she helped to save Jews from extermination in Austria during the Nazi occupation of Europe, but that is another chapter of her story. The final chapter occurred when she died on February 15th, 2001. Rose Freedman, quintessential New Yorker, smart, hard-working, made her own luck, and got lucky enough to live to the ripe old age of 107.

9

The Divine Right of Kings

There is an increasing tendency for the emergence of two Americas. There is the rich America, and then there is everyone else. The youth of rich America live in the world of private schools and tutors, and summer internships with the captains of industry in technology, finance, business, or philanthropy. It's no wonder that wealth and power are dynastic and get passed on from one generation to the next. The progeny of rich America get a different start in life from everyone else. When a man's first job out of college is interning for the former secretary of the treasury or the world's most successful hedge fund manager, he is leaping far ahead of everyone else. I have worked with clients whose children have never taken public transportation. Some have never flown on a commercial jet or have had to pass through airport security; they have only flown on private planes.

A "C-level" or "C-suite" position is nice work if you can get it. It's understandable why so many people want to be in the club. The salaries are astronomically high and the perks are amazing. But isn't it just ridiculous that CEOs still get paid egregious sums of money even when their performance is abysmal and they fail?

Bank of America once disclosed[35] it had $4 billion less in regulatory capital than it thought. Bank of America CEO Brian Moynihan called it a "disappointing mistake that the bank is investigating." He went on to say, "We continue to deliver on our strategy to make our company simpler, stronger, and more customer-driven." Whether the bank is in good position or not has no impact on Moynihan's earnings. As Bank of America's CEO, he received total compensation of $13.1 million in 2013. Chances are he will probably get an increase in earnings this year regardless of the $4 billon blunder.

Next time your checking account is overdrawn by $4, try contacting your bank to say "it is a disappointing mistake that your family is investigating." And then add, "We continue to deliver on our strategy to make our family simpler, stronger, and more value-driven."

There are other kings reigning in America. Another recent example is Goldman Sachs' award to its CEO Lloyd Blankfein of about $23 million in salary and bonus for 2013, which was an increase of about 9.5 percent from 2012. It's noteworthy that Mr. Blankfein was awarded a bonus of restricted stock of $14.7 million and a cash bonus of approximately $6 million in addition to his $2 million salary, even though revenue for Goldman Sachs was flat and there was a decline in compensation—for everyone else.

Mr. Blankfein's increase in salary allowed him to stay in the club with James "Jamie" Dimon of JPMorgan Chase and James Gorman, Morgan Stanley, who also received enormous stock awards from their companies, even more than the stock awards they earned from the previous year. Who could forget the media images of Jamie Dimon smiling sheepishly before the camera while trying to explain JPMorgan Chase's $5.8 billion trading loss?[36]

Why are these CEOs getting rewarded for losing billions of dollars? It is as if they can write the rules in their own favor. Even when they lose everyone else's money, they still come out on top.

The HR practices of many corporations devalue most employees and excessively reward C-suite executives even when they're aggressively stupid about running a company. The rationale behind paying so much money to C-executives is because they are irreplaceable, indispensable, and as infallible as the Pope. We know it's a scam and the game is rigged. Anyone can be replaced and it takes a team of great people working together to make a company thrive and prosper.

In his book *Management Challenges for the 21ˢᵗ Century*, Peter F. Drucker said, "We talk incessantly about teams—and every study comes to the conclusion that the top management does need a team. Yet, we now practice—and not only in

American Industry—the most extreme cult of CEO Supermen." The current accepted practice of CEO compensation operates with the same inclusiveness and built-in suite of privileges as a feudal monarchy. Today's CEOs command as though they've been imbued by birth with the Divine Right of Kings.

There is no hard data to indicate that paying egregiously high salaries to CEOs is a drain on the American economy. And yet the fact that people at the top echelons of corporate America get insanely rewarded for doing a bad job is terrible for our morale. Right now middle-class Americans are being heavily taxed without gaining anything in return for the amount of money they are paying into the system to support the basic infrastructure. If middle-class Americans paid the same rate of taxes as people in Scandinavian countries, they would be getting tons of services, including advanced health care and an exceptional standard of living. The Divine Right of Kings is making a mockery of the core values of who we are as Americans.

How can people take pride in their jobs when there is huge disparity between what they earn and what their leadership earns, especially when that leadership is incompetent? Complaining about the Divine Right of Kings on social media isn't going change the game. Getting recognition and reward for your hard work commands respect, and that is a game changer. The underlying drive of why we work hard is to experience the rewards of accomplishment. Everyone should be well paid for working hard and for being accomplished, not just CEOs. If you have to put your faith anywhere, place your bet on the American people. We fought the American Revolution to get rid of a tyrannical monarchy and we might have to do it again.

If you examine the news with a healthy skepticism and use your critical thinking skills, you will observe how frequently the media is rigged in favor of the captains of industry. Shortly after 9/11, there was one power broker who pressed on to favor his own self-interest even in the wake of great tragedy. Larry Silverstein, who was the leaseholder of the World Trade Center when it was destroyed, was interviewed in *The New York Times* four months after the destruction of the Twin Towers. He had much to say about the new buildings that would be erected in the place of the devastated site of the Twin Towers. The fires were still burning and bodies were still being carried out on flag draped stretchers, and yet Mr. Silverstein already had a plan for urban expansion.

The New York Times continued to report Mr. Silverstein's spin for the next few months following 9/11. By January 2002, Mr. Silverstein's contractors were breaking ground where Building 7 WTC had once stood. Moral to this story: grieving can only go on for so long when there is money to be made. Real estate developer Larry Silverstein has a net worth of $3.5 billion. Soon after Silverstein declared his intent to rebuild on the site of the World Trade Center, he and his insurers became embroiled in a dispute over whether the attacks on the Twin Towers had constituted one event or two "acts of terrorism" under the terms of the insurance policy. In 2007, the insurance settlement reached with insurers agreeing to pay out a total of $4.55 billion to Mr. Silverstein's holding company.[37]

Paul Krugman, American economist and op-ed columnist for *The New York Times*, reported incontrovertible evidence for the growing inequality of wealth in the United States—the widening gap between a small minority of the superrich and the rest of us. The statistics are alarming. Over the last 15 years, US census data shows a dramatic increase of income among the top 20 percent wealthiest American families, and within that group, it was actually the top 5 percent that reaped the highest gains in reported income. Krugman also reported there was a significant decrease going to families in the middle-income sectors among the shrinking middle class. A study conducted by the Congressional Budget Office found that between 1979 and 1997, the after-tax incomes of the top 1 percent of families rose 157 percent, compared with a 10 percent gain for families near the middle of the income distribution. A small number of the very, very rich now control the nation's wealth.

Krugman wrote his analysis, after the dot.com collapse, but years before the collapse of the sub-prime mortgage and housing markets, in his *New York Times* article "For Richer."[38] Since that time and during the long recession, the widening gap between the superrich and everyone else has intensified. Emmanuel Saez and Thomas Piketty, the two economists who have spent over a decade tracking the incomes of the poor, the middle class, and the rich, have found that the trends have mostly continued. From 2000 to 2007, incomes for the bottom 90 percent of earners rose only about 4 percent, once adjusted for inflation. For the top 0.1 percent, incomes climbed about 94 percent.

Many accomplished individuals are afraid to speak out about the mounting economic inequalities in American culture for fear of being labeled as radical, terrorist, or engaged in class warfare.[39] Class warfare exists when there are competing socioeconomic interests among people who belong to different economic classes. Remember, the only true American sin is telling the truth about corruption in a government, a company, or an organization in a way that challenges the status quo. Any criticism of the superrich is always positioned in the press as class warfare. The suggestion is that the less-than-wealthy are jealous of America's reigning class—the superrich. The reality is *class warfare* is a concept created by, perpetuated by, and actually coined by the more powerful economic class to create a gray area that obfuscates the increasing economic disparity.

When the widening economic disparity is spun as news in the press, it is often cited as the failure of the poor, working class, and middle class to be smart or industrious enough to achieve affluence. You will not find much investigative journalism probing the components of the financial infrastructure that has hardwired the game (jobs, tax structure, investments) in favor of the rich. It's no secret that investigative reporting (often defined as *real journalism*) has been on the decline ever since the media collapsed as an industry. Most media outlets no longer have the resources to allocate to investigative reporters to probe deeply in order to write fair, unbiased, and authentic news stories.

The numbers evidencing the widening economic gap between the rich and poor speak volumes.

The US Census Bureau report from 2012 shows one in four US residents live in "poverty areas." According to American Community Survey data collected by the US Census Bureau from 2008 to 2012, there was an increase from 2000, when less than one in five were reported to live in poverty. The number of people living in poverty areas increased from 49.5 million (18.0 percent) in 2000 to 77.4 million (25.7 percent) in 2008–2012. *More than half of people living in poverty lived in a poverty area, and about 30 percent of people living in poverty areas had incomes below the poverty level. "Researchers have found that living in poor neighborhoods adds burdens to low-income families, such as poor housing conditions and fewer job opportunities."* [40]

During the 1990s and until the crash of 2000, the number of individuals who invested in the stock market was unprecedented. We were led to believe we could all get rich. At one time, those who invested in the stock market were an exclusive club composed of the rich and the financially savvy. The once-exclusive club of investors dominated by the rich and financial experts opened up and became accessible to the great unwashed masses. Anyone could go online and for a nominal sum make a day trade.

Suddenly mail carriers, civil servants, longshoremen, beauty shop owners, and cashiers at Rite Aid were sharing stock tips the way one used to bet on horses at the track. We all played the stock market like gamblers full of bloodlust shooting craps in Las Vegas. A mood of buoyant mass hysteria prevailed: We believed we would get lucky and strike it big.

Who created the great American Gold Rush of the 1990s? The plutocracy of the Superrich? Our elected officials? Our appointed officials? Bankers? Venture capitalists? Self-proclaimed experts, pundits and financial analysts? The analysts fueled the frenzy and through the press told us to buy, hold, sell. Who paid the analysts? No one speaks frankly about who was welcomed inside the club and given privileged information, and who was left out in the cold. Why did business and financial media believe the analysts' spin and why did the press tell their story to manipulate the markets?

Don English, *The Idiot* CPA, mentioned earlier in *American Spin* as a strong example of *brand persona*, once described the lists as being made of a bell curve stratification just like a school class full of A, B, and C grades. Only in this case the ABCs had to do with who was going to make money in the markets and who would lose.

The A list—very exclusive, very rich—were tipped off when to get into the market and when to get out. (Martha Stewart, who was A list, was nabbed for being flagrantly careless. For reasons unknown, she is the fall guy for a whole club of superrich. Obviously she must have burst a bubble in someone's peach soufflé.)

The B list was told when to get in, but not necessarily when to get out. The B list are acquaintances to the A list but definitely not family or cherished friends.

The C list was not told when to get into the market or when to get out. The C list is everyone else in America: you, me, your dentist, your shrink, the working class, the upper middle class bent on retiring next year, and the kids next door who were putting away small monthly sums for their college funds.

In the end, it was the C list that bore the great brunt of the meltdown. A great transference of wealth took place. The superrich were able to cash in their options, netting huge profits that were funded from the general American public who blindly bought shares on a hunch or a whim—the C list. The A list skimmed off the top and made off with the booty while the great unwashed masses were left with dwindling savings.

The stock market in the late 1990s was an elaborate Ponzi scheme that had far reaching consequences. Wealth will always afford the P.R. and legal resources to fabricate a legal strategy as creative as the *Affluenza Defense*. A few choice personalities did take the fall for the failure of an entire company or corporate culture and did do time in white-collar penal facilities. You can hardly call them jails. An example of jail to the wealthy is house arrest in a $6.5 million dollar cooperative on the upper east side of Manhattan. Unless they had insider information, everyone who invested in the stock market lost money. And the majority of those who invested in the market did so without insider information.

Mostly everyone who did not have insider information was in the middle sector from the working poor/working class to the middle and upper middle class. Many lost their savings, 401k plans, and pension funds. Some lost their homes, their jobs, and their sense of self-worth. The dollars invested by the large burgeoning middle sector went solely to the A-list to pay them for their return on investment plus hefty profits. And it was all perfectly legal. It was only those exclusive members of the A-list who were given the opportunity—by virtue of their excellent connections—to skim from the top.

When the Enron scandal erupted in 2001, Edward Wyatt reported in *The New York Times* that credit-rating agencies, the independent security analysts that assess and pass judgment on a company's financial fitness, saw signs of Enron's deteriorating condition but did little to warn investors until at least five months later.[41] Long after the problems had emerged and Enron slid into bankruptcy was when the information became public information. The agencies? Moody's Investors Services, Standard & Poor's, and Fitch Ratings. The roles of the rating agencies, which are unregulated and consider themselves self-regulating professionals (accountants, lawyers, analysts, credit-rating agencies, and corporate entities), came under scrutiny, but in the end they got away with murder.

With Enron and all its financial ramifications, the fallout extending to corporations, accountants, analysts, lawyers, financial institutions, and individual Americans, there is a crisis of confidence that has beset our culture for over a decade. The past scandals surrounding the Enron phenomenon, which includes Global Crossing, Tyco International, Adelphia Communications, and then the next wave of financial collapse connected to real estate, mortgages, credit default swaps, collateralized mortgage obligations, and the downfall of Bear Stearns and Lehman Brothers, illustrate whether the trust people place in their employers, political leaders, and even the whole capitalist system of free trade is tragically misplaced. Religion, financial institutions, corporate America, government, our employers, and our leadership, all have failed us. Still, Americans want to believe in something, and they believe in the stories that are spun to the media by the divine kings.

Our divine kings are not benevolent despots who use their power and money to effect positive social reforms in healthcare or education to benefit the masses. Nor are our divine kings obvious tyrants who rule on whim and use extreme or overt violent tactics. Most divine kings are very aware of their public reputation and understand that perception must be managed. They do not want to be thought of as Michael Douglas playing the role of Gordon Gekko in the Hollywood film version of *Wall Street*. Gordon Gekko invests heavily in the stock market, futures, options, bonds, and real estate, and he says: "Greed is good, greed works." Gordon Gekko is eternally A-list; he will always have insider information. He knows when to get into the market and he knows when to get out. He will rarely get caught. If he does get caught, he will implement the best practices of *American Spin*. He will buy the best legal and P.R. counsel. He will get away with murder.

Even among the wealthiest captains of industry, there has been a call to action to address the growing economic disparity. There are divine kings who recognize the more serious consequences of the increasing economic disparity. By continuing to hamstring the poor, working, and middle classes, who will pay for America's infrastructure? According to the *2013 Report Card for America's Infrastructure*, the nation's infrastructure received a score of D-. The *Global Competitiveness Report for 2012-2013* indicated that the US has dropped seven slots in the global ranking of national infrastructure. If a majority of Americans continue to suffer from a decline in economic opportunity, who will pay taxes? Who will generate the tax revenue to pay for maintaining and upgrading the nation's crumbling bridges, tunnels, roads, and connective waterways? A discussion of the architectural, transportation, and logistics infrastructure is only the tip of the iceberg. There are many other ramifications related to how great economic disparity will impact the new business growth that needs to be sustained by a healthy and functioning middle class.

Warren Buffett, long considered to be one of the wealthiest investors of the world, has expressed his own concerns by calling on government legislators to stop coddling the superrich. Buffett cites the facts evidencing increasing inequality, especially when it comes to taxes. "Since 1992, the I.R.S. has compiled data from the returns of the 400 Americans reporting the largest income. In 1992, the top 400 had aggregate taxable income of $16.9 billion and paid federal taxes of 29.2 percent on that sum. In 2008, the aggregate income of the highest 400 had soared to $90.9 billion—a staggering $227.4 million on average—but the rate paid had fallen to 21.5 percent."[42]

Mr. Buffett must know that the destruction of the economic interests of those less than superrich can jeopardize the entire American infrastructure. After all, if the middle class does not bear the brunt of paying the taxes to support our basic government services, then the system can shut down. While Mr. Buffett is arguably the last person in the world who should care about the plight of the poor, working class, and middle classes, his public stance is brilliant positioning and well crafted spin. Keeping in mind that the best spin is always the truth, Mr. Buffett gives the perception that he is a champion of the middle class, and, at the same time, he is protecting his own interests. Among the superrich who are advocating for reforms in the tax structure, employment, or education, Mr. Buffett is not alone.[43] Mogul entrepreneurs such as George Soros have echoed similar populist sentiment in noteworthy spin.

George Soros, the chairman of Soros Fund Management, best-known as a speculator and a political activist, argued in his latest book, *The New Paradigm for Financial Markets*, that a "superbubble" has developed in the past 25 years and it is now collapsing. Even though he made a fortune by doing things such as betting against Britain's currency in 1992 and Thailand's in 1997, Soros, more than anything else, wants to be perceived as an economic philosopher. Since he was a student in 1952, he has been promoting his economic theory, which he calls "reflexivity." And since 1952, legions of academic economists have been dismissing his economic assertions and relegating his theory of reflexivity to the ranting of just another hedge fund manager's "write downs." Kudos to Soros for pressing on to be perceived as having an impact in solving the problems related to inherent economic inequality.

The Game is Rigged

Historically, America has been plagued with financial scandals. Some economists might cite the crash of Lehman Brothers in 2008 as the beginning of the current economic decline. Some experts believe it was the 1999 repeal of the Glass-Steagall Act that contributed to the financial crisis of 2008.[44]

There is no shortage of high profile scandals: Enron, Tyco International, Bernie Madoff; the list is long and includes one of the largest bankruptcies in American history—MF Global, a multinational futures broker and bond dealer. In its final days, former New Jersey Governor Jon Corzine was the CEO of MF Global when it was found that $1.6 billion of its customers' funds was missing. The money has never been recovered.

Six months before the Enron scandal broke during the summer of 2001, New York City suffered from massive power outages. Many areas of the country, California and the Pacific Northwest in particular, endured untold rate hikes for electrical power. The media told us en masse of the great energy crisis fueled by water shortages and antiquated utility infrastructures. Who spun these tales to the media? Every major utility company maintains sophisticated in-house corporate communications departments, not to mention the dollars spent to outsource media relations campaigns to the most expensive P.R. firms in the world—one more lesson in American spin. In the aftermath, we learned how Enron had completely rigged the utility markets, and through the use of artful spin, they were able to dupe everyone, including their own shareholders and the media.

Even now, we are still paying the price for Enron's crimes. Enron became a national symbol for the complete breakdown in trust people place in their leadership. With all of the hoopla that ensued from the Enron scandal, including congressional hearings, movie and book rights, and memorabilia available for sale on eBay, the only people who in fact paid the price for Enron's misdeeds are the people who are still paying exorbitant utility bills to heat their homes and keep the lights on.

Discussing the dot.com crash and older scandals such as Enron, Global Crossing, Tyco International, Adelphia Communications sounds like stale news when so much has since happened. The irony is the credit reporting agencies (CRAs) came back for a second act and played a critical role in the American subprime mortgage crisis of 2007–2008 that triggered the Great Recession of 2008–2009. The complex securities used to finance subprime mortgages could not have been sold without ratings by "The Big Three" CRAs—Moody's Investors Service, Standard & Poor's, and Fitch Ratings. The pools of debt the agencies gave their "triple-A" ratings included over three trillion dollars of subprime loans to homebuyers with bad credit and undocumented incomes. The losses came to over a half a trillion dollars, which led to the collapse of three investment banks—Bear Stearns, Lehman Brothers, and Merrill Lynch—and the federal governments buying of $700 billion of bad debt from distressed financial institutions in a bailout program (TARP), which ensures that everyone else—except for the superrich—will be paying back this debt for generations to come.

Enron may be old news, but the basic elements of what went wrong with Enron and its troubling economic impact on our economy have never been fixed. "The Big Three" continue to operate without penalty and little oversight, much the same way they did before the dot.com meltdown of 2000 and the collapse of the sub-prime mortgage market and ensuing recession in 2008. Despite the damage that impacted many Americans and the government infrastructure, for the top three credit reporting agencies it continues to be business as usual. If you do a routine search on the Internet seeking news about regulating or reorganizing the credit reporting agencies, you won't find any news. These captains of industry got away with murder.

America's spin or what we are led to believe about America is that it's a land of equal opportunity. We are led to believe: no matter how humble your origins are, you can still attain the American Dream. And exactly what is the American Dream? If the American Dream used to mean opportunity and freedom, then the new American Dream boils down to a single concept —money. In the new American Dream, opportunity and freedom can be obtained and experienced, but only with money. America is a free country but only if you have the money to afford liberty. If anyone thinks he is going to get rich quickly or easily, he needs to think again. The poor, disenfranchised, working poor, working class, or even the hamstrung middle and upper middle classes can no longer easily inherit the Divine Right of Kings.

While the kings admittedly have strong influence on the news and information disseminated in the media, they also use the media to harvest vast quantities of personal information about us. To some extent they can control the spin that is spewed to Americans based on our individual profiles on social media.

Can You Imagine Anyone Really Liking Goldman Sachs?

Recently, I was shopping for a new armchair to give as a present to my husband, so I used Google to search furniture websites. Now every time I go into my Facebook account, I see targeted ads for certain home décor companies and the photos of my Facebook friends who "like" them. Using the "likes" of my friends is not a huge selling point. For some of my friends, their idea of home décor is leaving their Christmas tree up until February because it adds a fresh burst of color to their living room.

In my Facebook, I also get targeted ads for shoes, cashmere sweaters, and skin care, even though there is nothing in my Facebook profile to indicate that I really do like these things. (I have searched for these items on Google and have purchased them online.)

I do know that the algorithms used by Facebook or Google are the function of the minds of engineers, and they have no way of telling which of my friends have intrinsic design sensibility that I might value. Soon algorithms will utilize a higher level of artificial intelligence and figure this out. And even when they do, I find it confusing to know which of my friends like something when all I want to do is look at chairs.

I'm not a geek, so I don't completely understand how, when I search for something on Google, Facebook harvests my information, so that algorithms will place pop-up ads on Facebook to sell me something I genuinely like. Maybe these two big players are actually more compatible with each other and cooperate more than they say they do. There is no clash of the titans. The technology giants are old-fashioned monopolies and oligarchies shaping our economic landscape in the age of communications the same way the railroads shaped the landscape in the age of industrialization at the beginning of the last century. Back then, a few players made a whole lot of money, and it is clear that history is repeating itself.

How do the kings control us? By harvesting the information we willingly place on social media and by controlling the spin that is fed to us through the media, the kings have amassed the power to reign indefinitely.

Next time you use Facebook, examine some of the amazing and improbable popularity of the Facebook fan pages that belong to large financial entities. Unbeknownst to many users of social media, P.R. professionals use many techniques to falsely inflate the numbers of fans on Facebook and followers on Twitter.

Morgan Stanley, who led the IPO for Facebook, is quite popular on Facebook, and the last time I checked it had 25,876 likes.

And Goldman Sachs, who gave Facebook a huge infusion of cash in anticipation of their IPO, is also very popular on Facebook. The last time I checked, Goldman Sachs has two fan pages, one for the bank and financial institution with 53,297 likes. Goldman Sachs also has a separate fan page for the organization with 88,885 likes. By the time you check these numbers for yourself, there will be many more new followers and fans.

As much as I have cautioned clients, colleagues, family and friends about being prudent and to exercise good judgment about what to post on Facebook or any other social media platform, I am constantly amazed by the embarrassing things people put out there for the whole world to see. This whole world that can access your information is composed of banks, lending institutions, insurers, employers, healthcare organizations, government institutions, and law enforcement. And if you think that your privacy settings will protect you from the predatory nature of the algorithms, then you deserve to be called a lemming looking to jump from the highest cliff.

In light of Facebook's giant status in technology and given the nature of the money backing the company, our personal information will be forever repackaged, repurposed, and sold to any company who wants to buy it. We will see how our personal information can be used without our consent for someone else's profit and gain, or later on, for even darker motives. Remember, algorithms have no heart. Be careful what you show, post, like, and say. Lemmings never see the edge of the cliff until it's too late.

In *Propaganda*, Edward Bernays wrote, "The conscious and intelligent manipulation of the organized habits and opinions of the masses is an important element in democratic society. Those who manipulate the unseen mechanism of society constitute an invisible government which is the true ruling power of our country." An oft-quoted sentiment of American lore states: he who has the gold makes the rules. The regulations regarding employment, taxes, healthcare insurance, and fundamental living expenses related to food, clothing, and shelter, are made to benefit the interests of rich Americans who can afford to pay for lobbyists, legions of lawyers and P.R. professionals. America is a land of fairness and equal opportunity, but the laws of our land will always be architected in favor of the Divine Right of Kings.

10

Paying Homage to the Head Beagle

Fleeing the fascism and corruption of Sicily, my grandfather, Joe Vaccarino, entered the US through Ellis Island. He lived on Mott Street in New York City's *Little Italy*, which is now part of Chinatown. Back in the day, Grandpa Joe hung out on the street. He played kick-the-can and bocce ball. Eventually, he moved uptown to the Bronx and later to Yonkers. He was a money lender, a *spalloni*, one of those who moves money. *La Stessa Cosa*. A man of honor. By the standards of today, he would simply be called a hedge fund manager.

Grandpa Joe was part of the immigrant culture that made New York City great. His friends were from all walks of life and came from all religions and ethnic groups. He lived the following creed: *I help you. You help me. We all rise together*.

Now we are all strangers wandering in a strange land. The changing global economy has made us immigrants in the new world order. Some people are throwing out all of the old ways of doing things. Others are stubbornly resistant to the changes taking place and insist on doing the same old things the same old way, even when it is clear that these methods no longer work, when a more prudent course of action is finding the right way to blend the old with the new. A new populism is rising, and now, more than ever, there is a great need to help one another.

Grandpa Joe didn't just rise up out of poverty and become an overnight success on his own accord. He had a little help from his friends. In every network, industry, trade, profession, sector, town, city, or organization there is a key influencer who is the reigning power and has the power to give someone a *come up*. And contrarily a key influencer has the power to take someone down. I refer to the key influencer—him or her, as the case may be—as *the head beagle*. There are head beagles everywhere. I never know when I might run into the head beagle. In terms of being a P.R. professional and a natural connector, it is my job to find and make contact with head beagles.

Those of you who know me, professionally or personally, know that I don't have a tendency to run at the mouth. I prefer to choose my words very deliberately. It's a personality trait that is at the core of my brand persona as a P.R. professional. On many occasions, I am required to keep information confidential about all of my clients, including past clients. There are some secrets I am sworn never to tell anyone. I have good reason to keep my mouth shut. My favorite Sicilian proverb goes something like this: one who speaks little makes mistakes. Imagine the one who speaks a lot.

Anyone of Sicilian heritage can attest that Sicilians are a funny people when it comes to talking too much. And I don't mean funny in the humorous sense. I mean funny like peculiar. I knew one person with the name of Vaccarino who was whacked, and his manner of death indicated that he talked too much. He had violated *Omerta*, the Sicilian code of silence.

Remember the Godfather? The dominant brand attribute exhibited by Vito Corleone is he didn't talk too much. A gesture with his hand, a raised eyebrow, and the smallest simple physical movements were great evidence of his brand strength. What he didn't say was sometimes more important than what he actually did say. And when he did talk, the room grew deathly quiet; everyone gave him their rapt attention and listened. Even if iPhones had been around, no one would have been checking their messages. When planning your P.R. campaigns, it's not a bad idea to be strategic and to think like a clever Sicilian. Put the lid on your big mouth. What you say as well as what you don't say can make a lasting impression about you and your professional brand for years to come.

The Godfather knew how to build a network. Keep in mind that the concept of "The Godfather" is not a singularly male phenomenon. Mario Puzo claimed to have created the Godfather character Vito Corleone modeled after his own mother. The

Godfather, regardless of gender, knows how to surround himself with a close-knit circle of allies, strategic partnerships, and key influencers—head beagles—who understand this guiding principle: *I help you. You help me. We all rise together.*

People must use spin and P.R. tools to help grow their careers and businesses. As with all things, there is good spin and bad spin, good personal reputations and bad reputations. P.R. is much more than the discipline of getting along with others, building community, selling goods or services, getting elected for political office, or getting media coverage. Good P.R. is about getting the right message out to the people whom you want to hear what you have to say—your desired target audience. More importantly, practicing good P.R. means connecting with the right people and creating the right network so you can get what you want out of business and life.

Every industry has a head beagle or two, or several. Most head beagles do not show up at business networking events. They don't have the time and they don't like being swarmed by insufferable glad-handers who want something for nothing. The beagle knows the real rules—the hidden rules that aren't posted on any website. The head beagle doesn't like email. He doesn't do social media. He doesn't leave a digital trail. He doesn't want to get sued. He doesn't want to get killed. He doesn't want to lose business. Above all else, he doesn't want to lose his power. He's the guy who says: *why didn't you pick up the phone and call me?*

The term and concept of a *head beagle* is derived from the world of old money and old family connections. I coined the term when I read an article, written by Caitlin Macy, a wedding announcement that was reprinted from the Sunday, Feb 3, 2002, *New York Times* wedding section. The wedding announcement pertained to the marriage of David Sloan and Judith Place.[45] It is hard to believe that there is a world of old money and old family connections in America that prevails even in the postmodern era. Here is an example of old money that evidences how not only does an old rich plutocracy still exist, but it actually flourishes in this postmodern age in an almost suspended state of altered reality that seems to be unreal—and yet it is unequivocally real and true.

Both David Randolph Sloan and Judith Gauntlett Place grew up in Millbrook, New York. With a deep abiding attachment to horsemanship, beagling, and a preppy brand of elitism, both went to toney private schools. Judith Place had attended Miss Porter's School and David Sloan went to Millbrook School. They even worked for seven years in the same office building in Stamford, Connecticut. Mr. Sloan, a post-Cold-War uranium trader, often traveled to Kazakhstan and Uzbekistan. Ms. Place was partner in the accounting firm Deloitte & Touche. Their paths in life were fairly parallel, yet they had never met. On their first date, they went beagling in Millbrook, where they both had a family network going back generations. (Ms. Place's grandfather had helped establish Millbrook as a weekend retreat. One of Mr. Sloan's ancestors had founded the Millbrook Hunt.) The day after their wedding, they took their guests beagling, and wearing "knee breeches and field coats, the new Mr. And Mrs. Sloan charged up the hill after the pack, the bridegroom shouting, 'Never give up the high ground!'"

Mr. Sloan's occupation as a post-Cold-War uranium trader who often traveled to Kazakhstan and Uzbekistan stands out. You will not see a post in the classifieds, on Craig's List, or in an executive search firm recruiting for a post-Cold-War uranium trader. How Mr. Sloan got his job has more to do with beagling and the head beagle. Unlike most Americans, he was bred to beagle and he was wired into a network that provided him with the unusual opportunities that are only offered to those who are rich, entitled and bestowed with the Divine Right of Kings.

Soon we will deal with the power of connectivity, networking, and the concept of not what you know but whom you know, and we will place it within its correct frame of reference through the lens of *American Spin*.

Being a head beagle is not an honorary title limited to the horsey set and old money. There are head beagles everywhere from Millbrook, New York, to the South Bronx. Remember the Godfather? He was the ultimate head beagle and he knew how to build a network. Nothing is accomplished in America without networking, without utilizing whom you know as a resource, and finding out whom you still need to know. Introductions count. Recommendations and referrals are paramount. We are not of a royal class where every connection and contact has already been preordained by bloodlines for centuries. In America, every class, every profession, every industry, every aspect of American culture, including all aspects of its subculture from WASPs and Goths to Fundamentalist Christians and Homies, has its own business and social network. Every network is made up of the right contacts that must be cultivated in order to get that job, get that movie role, get that promotion, to gain admission into school, entrance into your favorite club, restaurant, or organization, to get that big break, to build a business, and to build a good name.

Who counts? The most important tool a P.R. professional has is a network. Your network can be your little address book, the contacts in your LinkedIn, or all the names and numbers you carry around in your head. Paper, pen, electronic... the platform of your network is inconsequential. What matters is the depth and breadth of your personal and professional network. You don't need to work in P.R. to have a powerful network that relates directly to your own brand and reputation. Everyone needs to cultivate contacts. And it goes without saying that some networks are more powerful than others. I define networking as the lifelong accumulation of all contacts relevant to positioning yourself favorably in the world you live in, whether your world is the south Bronx or Kennebunkport, Maine.

Your family background does matter. How much money you are born into or where you go to school also matters. This testimony was posted on a website by Harvard University alumna: "Do not underestimate the power and prestige of this institution—getting into Harvard is a golden ticket that gives you the power to go practically anywhere you choose. Harvard has given me the room to stretch myself out and to become more than I ever guessed that I could be."

Don't ever underestimate the power of *who you know*. A former colleague of mine, *who I will refer* to as *Amanda Spier*, speaks on a daily basis of her MBA from Harvard. She plays this Ivy League shtick over and over because it is a trump card—her primary asset. The MBA from Harvard has enabled Amanda to stay gainfully employed even in times of woeful economic downturn. She has said frequently and quite ruefully, "It isn't what you know, it is who you know." I concurred with her assessment with one minor adjustment; it is not only whom you know, but *whom you know* must be coupled with *what you know*." Sooner or later everyone is found out for the level of talent they can bring to the party, regardless of whether or not you were wired-in and born on third base.

Since 1996, Amanda Spier has had a long string of jobs, twelve in all. Each stint lasted a year or less, sometimes only six months. She knows how to schmooze her Ivy League cronies into helping her get employed but not keep her job. Even the head beagle cannot save you from your own lackluster self forever. It's never only about whom you know; more importantly, it's about how well you perform with the opportunity you have been given.

Here is a story about two literary agents, one moneyed and wired, and the other not. Lana DiOrio is big, loud, brash, and from Brooklyn. She graduated from Marymount College, a small all girls' Catholic college in New York. The other agent, Ellen White, is an insipid WASP who disdains make-up, is fond of penny loafers, and attended Smith College. Lana DiOrio and Ellen White have had a bitter rivalry for years. Their operating styles could not be more different. Lana DiOrio is loud, generous, and used to hitting the ground running like a Mack truck. She's been known to use her mouth like it's a dangerous weapon. Ellen White wrinkles her nose with disdain at the slightest dose of impropriety, and that includes everything south of Bar Harbor, Maine.

My prominent British literary author friend is mortally offended by the loutish sensibility of Lana DiOrio and speaks of her disrespectfully, as if she was a working class call girl instead of a literary agent. During our discourses on good, evil, and sin, he has called her a piece of work and the devil incarnate. Lana is just too rough, too coarse, too Brooklyn for his taste. Instead he extols the virtues of Ellen White. He says Ellen has real connections in the New York publishing world and she has worked really hard to get them. Ellen White might have great connections, but she just didn't have to work too hard to get them. Ellen White's husband had roomed at Harvard with Joe Kennedy during a time when Jackie Onassis was still alive and ensconced at Doubleday. Not a bad start for a first connection in publishing. Working class girl Lana DiOrio's first connection has always been, and will always be, her mouth.

Anytime you hear of someone who easily achieved success, probe further for the truth. More often than not, you will find the particular someone came with papers issued by the head beagle and had the wheels greased. It's like Maureen Dowd's comment about George W. Bush. Ms. Dowd implied that "W" acted like he scored a home run, when in reality he was born on third base.* If you're not A-list from the onset, you will have to work a whole lot harder and smarter just to get to par.

Jack Grubman, formerly a top telecom and technology analyst at Salomon Smith Barney, the investment-banking division of Citigroup, sought the help of Sanford "Sandy" Weill to get his young twins admitted to the 92nd Street Y. Many captains of industry believe that the "Y" will facilitate an easier acceptance to Harvard for toddlers who begin school there, and there is some substance behind the belief. It's been rumored that statistically it's easier to get into the Harvard freshman class than it is to get into preschool at the 92nd Street Y. At a critical juncture in the preschool admissions process, Jack Grubman raised the rating of a stock in AT&T, which was at that time a potential

---

*Ann Richards said this about George Bush, senior, in 1988. And, the quote is actually attributed to Barry Switzer.

http://en.wikiquote.org/wiki/Ann_Richards

Citigroup client. In the meantime, through the efforts of Sandy Weill, Citigroup donated a million dollars to the 92nd Street Y. Coincidentally, Jack Grubman's twins were accepted by the nursery school.[46]

Jack Grubman's influence peddling to get his twins admission into the 92nd Street Y Nursery School struck a powerful chord that sparked controversy and stirred up resentment based on class distinction and class envy. It reminded many people of the unfairness, and just how the wealthy manage to rig the game board against the rest of us. The 92nd Street Y is also a strong metaphor to give instruction in the power of networking. Sandy Weil influenced a million dollar donor gift for the enrichment of Jack Grubman's children. Powerful and important men like Jack Grubman and Sanford Weil take the prospect of getting into the right network seriously, because they are head beagles. They decide who gets in and who does not get an opportunity.

You can be anything you want to be has traditionally been considered a wise American adage to tell children so they would be made aware of their unlimited potential and feel empowered. Reality, however, intrudes. The suggestion that you can be anything you want to be borders on the slightly ridiculous. Women don't get to be linebackers for the Dallas Cowboys, the blind do not get hired as graphic designers, the deaf do not become sound engineers, and on a more pragmatic level, kids from Bed-Sty in Brooklyn do not learn how to beagle in Millbrook, New York. The truth is you can be anything you want to be in those worlds that will claim you as belonging to and being one of *them.*

Ask Yourself: What Will You Do For the Head Beagle?

Everyone must build the right network. One way to build the right network is to pay homage to the head beagle. It does not matter if you are an accountant, an attorney, doctor, dentist, or even an author. You need to identify the head beagles (there are many) in your life and business and find a way to connect with them. Most people approach the head beagle with their hat in hand asking for a favor. Ask yourself: who is the head beagle in your world? Consider how many requests she must get every day from people who want something from her. And most of the time, they want something for nothing.

One scene in the movie *The Godfather* shows the procession of people lined-up to seek favors from the Don on the day of his daughter's wedding. Every Sicilian approached the Don with a unique request. Each story had a spin, a message, and was carefully crafted to have a hook and to keep some facts in the story and to leave some out. Asking for favors is a customary art form in the Sicilian culture. Even though the Sicilians were asking for favors from Don Corleone, they understood the unspoken rule. They knew one day, at any given time, the Don would come to ask them for a favor to pay him back.

In the American culture, there are many people in business who do not understand that Don Corleone himself could have written the fundamental laws of power. *The Godfather* is a great metaphor for life and business. Most people approach the head beagle asking for favors and a *come up*—for nothing. They don't seem to get the fact that they need to provide value. You need to let the head beagle know exactly what you can do for him now or what you will provide for him at some time in the future when you are called upon to return the favor. When you craft spin for the head beagle, you need to be able to communicate the value you will bring to the relationship.

Over the Rainbow and Over the Top

By paying homage to the head beagles in your world, will inevitably invite a higher rate of success for your endeavors. Take the author Thomas Pynchon. Thomas Pynchon's *Gravity's Rainbow* is not my favorite book. I especially dislike the book for being so long and completely unintelligible. Several times throughout my life, I struggled to get past the first fifty pages of *Gravity's Rainbow* to get a sense of story or character, and there was only raging madness about bananas, breasts, and rockets. The story and language cannot be tracked by any reader well enough to be understood, yet the book has received monumental critical acclaim.

James Joyce's *Ulysses* presents an equally compelling case for the concept of incoherent stream-of-consciousness masquerading as great literature. Both James Joyce and Thomas Pynchon achieved amazing success because they had tapped into the right network of people who created a powerful cult and mystique around the authors and their works. Claiming these works are exceptional, even though they are not, is the essence of when knowing the hand of the head beagle is inextricably linked to the spin that gets written up in the press. It is the word of the head beagle that will inevitably open the right doors to critics, influencers (other head beagles), and the press.

I, too, can be a sucker for bad spin. If I could not appreciate these masterful tales the way one would develop a fine palate for caviar or exquisite truffles, then the fault was mine. I was the idiot, not Thomas Pynchon or James Joyce. If you use the strength of your own perceptions and your own reasoning without listening to nonsense, then certain truths prevail. The job of a writer is to communicate, not to obfuscate. A great writer creates a great work or *magnum opus* when the reader is drawn into the story and able to care enough about the characters to form a lasting emotional bond. No one cares about Molly Bloom in *Ulysses*, and I can't remember the name of Pynchon's main character or even determine if there is one.

Ralph Waldo Emerson, who is truly a gifted writer, stated in his essay *Self-Reliance*, "In every work of genius we recognize our own rejected thoughts; they come back to us with a certain alienated majesty." Ultimately, a magnum opus moves us emotionally because we are able to experience another side of humanity and identify with this new discovery and find the common denominator within our own selves. We become one with the story and care about what happens to the characters. A great book creates a powerful emotional connection with its readers and ultimately has the power to transform lives.

The amount of P.R. attention given to Thomas Pynchon and James Joyce is exceptional and yet *Gravity's Rainbow* and

Ulysses do not hit the mark of a *magnum opus*. At least one literary critic, Richard Ellmann, built his entire career as a critic on the back of James Joyce's work.

There are literary experts who have steered far from the herd of hype. Author Max Eastman categorized James Joyce along with Gertrude Stein and T.S. Eliot among the "Unintelligibles," and Harvard Professor Irving Babbitt dismissed *Ulysses* as a book that could only have been written "in an advanced stage of psychic disintegration."[47] And in 1974, a three-member jury on fiction nominated *Gravity's Rainbow* for the Pulitzer Price for Fiction. Eleven other members of the board, however, overturned this decision and that year no award was given for fiction rather than giving the Pulitzer Prize to Thomas Pynchon for *Gravity's Rainbow*.

I have known brilliant writers who are as unintelligible as Thomas Pynchon and James Joyce, but most of them are muttering to themselves and working as night janitors in cheap hotels. Sadly unknown but talented people toil away at their craft, rarely thinking about whom they need to meet to become recognized for their talent. Sometimes they do have an inkling that they could use an influencer or two in their lives, but they are short on emotional intelligence and say all the wrong things to the right people and always at the wrong time. They lack a glib tongue, a sense of timing, and an innate flair for spin and P.R. They might know how to craft truly fine writing but they don't know how to craft spin.

Thomas Pynchon and James Joyce, on the other hand, are masters of P.R. James Joyce found his perfect advocate in Gertrude Stein, who had profound influence on the careers of luminaries ranging from Ernest Hemingway to Pablo Picasso. Thomas Pynchon is married to top literary agent Melanie Jackson, who recently negotiated his ebook deal. Ms. Jackson, by the way, is a great-granddaughter of Theodore Roosevelt and a granddaughter of US Supreme Court Justice Robert H. Jackson. Surely, her pedigree ensures powerful contacts among notable head beagles.

Pynchon has a fully engaged business network of influencers who stand to benefit by knowing him. Years ago, Pynchon's literary colleague Salman Rushdie was sentenced to death by Muslim extremists for writing *The Satanic Verses*. Rushdie's book was perceived to be sacrilegious by Muslim fundamentalists, so they sentenced Salman Rushdie to death. Although Thomas Pynchon is a self-proclaimed recluse, in a moment of supreme extroversion, Pynchon jumped headfirst into the middle of the Fatwah and wrote public letters of support for Salman Rushdie and his book *The Satanic Verses*. Pynchon's fourth novel *Vineland* disappointed most fans and critics. But who should cover his back? None other than Salman Rushdie. Incredible as it may seem, the nagging P.R. voice inside of me has always wondered whether Salman Rushdie (or his P.R. person) staged his own *fatwah* controversy. After all, the Ayatollah Khomeini is dead and there is no telling. Keep in mind, the rumor that circulated soon after Rushdie insulted the Islamic world, was that his next book was going to be called *Buddha, You Big Fat Fuck*.

As a true master of spin, Pynchon claims he does not like to talk to the press, and he refuses to make public appearances, yet he made two cameo animated appearances on the popular television show *The Simpsons*. Pynchon fancies himself as a recluse, but he sure knows how to network! It takes a full-out and sustaining P.R. campaign to make sure that everyone in the world knows you like to hide indoors. His turgid insistence on maintaining his privacy resulted in wild rumors suggesting he was the Unabomber or a member of the Waco Branch Davidian. Now really, how did those funny rumors manifest themselves in the first place?

When *Gravity's Rainbow* won the National Book Award, Pynchon would not accept the award. His publisher asked the Comedian Irwin Corey to accept the award on Pynchon's behalf. During Corey's acceptance speech, a streaker crossed the stage. I wonder, who hired the streaker?

Thomas Pynchon's resistance to fame reminds me of the time I was having dinner with another famous, but unnamed, British literary author who told me he wanted a large social media presence, but he did not want anyone to know that he was behind it. He wanted the social media following to appear instantly and as if he was so fabulous that throngs of people sought him out for no other reason than to be his fan.

At the end of the day, examining Thomas Pynchon and James Joyce is not about the books or their authors; it's about the power of P.R. and the necessity of having key influencers in your lives. Without having an extraordinary and powerful network in place, both of these gents would be lucky to find jobs bussing tables in the back room restaurant of a cheap hotel.

Throughout my career in P.R., I have represented clients, some of whom have impeccable credentials and some who have no credentials at all, and I have found that those who aggressively promote themselves will be the voices that are ultimately recognized and heard. Today's public is more likely to listen to bloggers rather than to poets and intellectuals who in the past have been considered our chief visionaries, change agents, and the protectors of innovative thinking.

No one listens to poets and academics any longer, which is indeed a sad state of affairs. When President Obama appointed the Pulitzer Prize winning poet Philip Levine as the poet laureate, most Americans had never heard of him. It was evident Philip Levine's major form of P.R. outreach was forming lasting relationships with his own powerful network—one reason why he became known enough to be awarded the honor of *poet laureate*. He certainly had not reached out to the media or to the people. Of course his poetry was fine, but there are many good poets, and not all of them have a strong network of head beagles.

What I'm about to say has little to do with books, business, poetry, or academia, and everything to do with striking the right chord with the right people at the right time. It's about being in the right network in your chosen profession, no matter what that profession might be, whether you're a shoemaker, a graphic designer, an actor, a CPA, or an author. You can't achieve stellar success unless the right people believe in your talent and your competence. People are only willing to believe in your greatness when they stand to benefit from knowing you. All of which brings us back to the value of *The Godfather* concept. Head beagles are not magnanimous caregivers doling out influence for free. There is always something in it, tangible or not, for the head beagle.

In his book *Propaganda,* Edward Bernays wrote about influencers and asked the following, "Who are the men, who, without our realizing it, give us our ideas, tell us whom to admire and whom to despise, what to believe about the ownership of public utilities, about the tariff, about the price of rubber, about the Dawes Plan, about immigration; who tell us how our houses should be designed, what furniture we should put into them, what menus we should serve at our table, what kind of shirts we must wear, what sports we should indulge in, what plays we should see, what charities we should support, what pictures we should admire, what slang we should affect, what jokes we should laugh at?" Bernays also noted: "we do not often stop to think that there are dictators in other fields whose influence is just as decisive as that of the politicians...."

Build Your Own Mafia

Don Corleone said, "Choose your friends well, but choose your enemies even more carefully." It is important to strategically choose your enemies for two reasons. Your enemies will define your persona with greater power and clarity than many of your friends. Your enemies will also define your network. As you move forward and win the favor of head beagles, you will be able to focus on winning alliances and partnerships with *friends of friends* and easily dismiss anyone connected with an enemy.

As a human being, inevitably you will make enemies. And this is a good thing. It is important to repel those influencers who will never be your ally and who will never do anything for you. By defining your enemies, you are putting a stake in the ground. It is always your choice, however, to decide who your enemy will be. Just because someone wronged you, it does not mean they will automatically become your enemy. It is your response to the "wrongful action" that will define whether the wrongdoer becomes your enemy. On some occasions, it is more fitting with your persona to overlook, forgive, or reconcile with the wrongdoer. Don Corleone, the Godfather, always saw the big picture: Petty grievances and turf wars get in the way of doing business.

The scene in *The Godfather* when Don Corleone says, "I hold my friends close to my heart, but I hold my enemies even closer," speaks precisely about the true nature of American business. At times it is best to cooperate and collaborate with your enemy. Don't mistake cooperation or collaboration for friendship. In these situations, temporary strategic alliances are a means to an end. If need be, sleep with the enemy. Throw cold water on your face and get over it. In the end, it's all about making your numbers and meeting your P.R. objectives.

Create your own mafia. This is America. There are tons of networks. Get to know *those who know* in the networks that are important to you. Make contacts. Engender relationships. Offer benefit and expect benefit in return. Create your own terms, bargain each term, and make your intentions known. Draft your contract in blood, an inviolable and implicit understanding of what each person should gain from the deal. Please note: no paper should exchange hands. This is a handshake deal. If the contract does not meet your expectations, walk away. There is no such thing as a deal so great that it cannot be passed up. There is always a better deal with a better contact that can be found.

Your degree does matter, and so does your pedigree, your ethnicity, and your religion. Remember the lesson of the fickle head beagle. You don't get to be a post-Cold-War uranium trader in Kazakhstan and Uzbekistan if you grow up on the wrong side of 8 Mile, Detroit. With talent, hard-won luck, and true grit you do get the shot to be Eminem. Whatever world you live in, you owe it to yourself to make it work for you. You have to understand your world and define the outer boundaries of its territory so you know how far you can expand your network. Whatever world you live in, you owe it to yourself to be well connected. It takes time, talent, and discipline to make and keep contacts. Make your network your finest tool and your prized possession. Go on, right now, connect with the head beagles you need to know and offer to bring value. This is America, a place of many worlds. Remember Rose Freedman who networked herself to the roof of a burning building and made it out alive.

11

How To Be a Master or Look Just Like One

Good P.R. is essential to the growth and viability of any business or any individual. Most entrepreneurs cannot afford to pay for a P.R. firm or pay for advertising and sponsorship, which now masquerades as authentic news stories. Now I invite you to explore the following question: How can you as an entrepreneur run a strong P.R. campaign? Some people think good P.R. is simply sending out press releases to a press list and you or your company becomes instantly famous. Others know P.R. is very complicated, requires intense focus, persistence, dedication, time, money, and its strategy is tantamount to an all-out military offensive that is meant to win a war.

If you have talent, and you are unknown, how will you become known for who you are and what you do? Whom do you need to know? Who will benefit from knowing you? How will you reach the people you need to know? If you believe you have talent, and if you believe you have a reputation that is worthy of recognition, then you must ask yourself, *how will I achieve the accolades and respect of head beagles in order to catapult myself to the highest level—to that of a master?*

How do individuals and entrepreneurs choose the right P.R. tools to build their brand, manage their reputation, and attain the level of a master? There are a ton of how-to articles out there that offer rote guidance. For example, many how-to articles suggest becoming a thought leader and writing press releases. What does this mean? The world doesn't need another boring article summarizing five ways to improve your elevator speech or eight ways to retain great employees. If you take a quick scan of the business how-to articles on LinkedIn, many appear to be thinly veiled plagiarism—the same old recycled content. Another factor to consider is that the press release is dead. In today's clutter, entrepreneurs who are inexperienced in how P.R. works will waste their time by writing press releases. The great majority of press releases are summarily ignored by the media and do not get placed as news.

Entrepreneurs and individuals must invest in core P.R. tools that, if utilized properly over time, will sustain the growth of your business. In my experience, the P.R. tools that you select must be the right P.R. tools for you, your profession, and your industry. You need to choose the tools that feature your strengths and minimize your weakness.

P.R. Tools for Individuals and Entrepreneurs

Media Relations is the most crucial part of any master-building strategy. It can take individuals to unforeseen heights, create new trends, and build innovative markets. Getting placed in the media is still a major way to gain credibility as a master. Reach out to the journalists who cover your field to let them know you are available for commentary when they need a source. Use services that will connect you with the press. Be truthful about the best media outlets for your news coverage. Don't use video if you do not present well on camera. Don't do radio if you don't have a pleasing voice or can't fluidly articulate your opinions. Stick with the forms of media that are the most flattering to your overall persona, talent, and expertise.

What is news? How is news spread? In 1928, Edward Bernays stated, "Instead there are numerous other media of communication, some new, others old but so transformed that they have become virtually new. The newspaper, of course, remains always a primary medium for the transmission of opinions and ideas—in other words, for propaganda."

Almost a century later in a mind-numbing digital age, there is still no greater credibility for you or your business than getting authentic news coverage. There is more media than ever and these media outlets range from the equivalent of 3-pound dumbbells to the bench press. To get a larger audience, you want to shoot for top-tier press. Let's take two heavyweight contenders—*The New York Times* and *Tech Crunch*. How do you get in? There are three must-do rules to get into top-tier press: research your editors and writers, develop a long-term relationship with key journalists, and, before you pitch a journalist, always make sure you have a good story.

Research Your Editors and Writers

You wouldn't go into a business meeting without knowing something about the person you are meeting with. Why should it be any different with a journalist? Track reporters who cover news relevant to you and your business. You don't necessarily need to access the databases used by P.R. professionals. Internet research can cover a lot of ground and provide you with most journalists' recent articles and posts. You should be able to see how long the journalist has covered a beat and get a handle on his writing style, pet peeves and specific areas of coverage.

Develop a Long-Term Relationship

Before you even pitch a story, start by laying some groundwork. Send each journalist-of-interest an email with your brief bio or electronic press kit. Introduce yourself. Compliment her work and tell her why. Open a dialogue. Build a relationship. Stay in touch by email on a monthly basis. Comment on her news stories even if you did not participate. If you see a story in the news that speaks to your expertise, then immediately email or call the journalist and let her know you are available for interview, if not this time, then maybe next time. You must connect with journalists. You are savvy enough to know that sending a press release can be a complete waste of time. Instead, connect with journalists by letting them know about your expertise and how you can help. Focus on reaching key influencers or journalists who are the most likely to need you. Stay in touch. Make yourself indispensable, so reporters will want to call you.

You Must Have a Good Story

You must be brutally honest with yourself. Do you really have a good story? Many CEOs fall prey to hubris and think the most trivial event involving them has the makings for the first page of *The New York Times* business section. Remember the Big Kahuna and his flawed set of expectations for what constituted a good news story? Always ask: does your news cover the latest trends in technology in a compelling story that has not been told before? Do your research and gather the numbers and datasets that support your story. To frame your news, are you willing to say positive things about your competitors? Are you such an expert on the topic that people pay you for your opinions? If you can answer yes to all of these questions, then it may be worth a pitch to the heavyweights.

You can place a story with just a hook and the spin, but a truly great story has all four elements: the hook, the spin, the heart, and the soul.

Hook is the angle that reeled you in and got your attention. It is the headline grabber and what you see in the newspapers every day. State your most exciting news in as few words as possible. Create a dramatic and powerful lead sentence—this is your hook.

Spin is the art of telling a story. Spin is composed of the facts you put into the story and the facts you purposefully omitted. It is also how you have layered the facts—the precise order of how you revealed information. Every story needs characters, people, good guys, bad guys, a location or sense of place, conflict, climax, and resolution. As the story evolves, what keeps your attention? There is no room for hype, but never let the facts get in the way of a good story.

Heart. How do the characters connect with their audience? What do the characters have in common with the audience? Does the audience empathize with the characters in the story? What emotions does the story conjure? Do people care? Why should they care? When in doubt, throw in cute animals or animated characters.

Soul. This is the most challenging aspect of a story. Is the story rich enough in emotional content to connect with any human being? Does the story have universal appeal? Does the story make a difference in someone's life?

Effective storytelling requires training and practice. Your pitch needs to be an excellent conversation. You should lay the groundwork by putting together a pitch that covers all of the salient points of your story. A well thought-out pitch is essential. You must always make certain that the content of your pitch is consistent with the key messages in the overall brand for you or your business, and yet at the same time, it's genuinely a great story! Placing a story and making news for your company must always be consistent with your overall P.R. strategy and the core focus of your business.

What Would the Head Beagle Think?

P.R. is much more than getting consistent media coverage; it's about keeping your name in front of *the head beagle*. Good P.R. is developing the highest number of high quality relationships that span across industries and sectors to get you a return on investment. When I say *investment*, I don't mean only money. I am also referring to time. Time is the one asset that once you give it away, you can't get it back. It's gone forever. In the post-modern world of massive clutter, everyone would agree that time is our number one resource. There are multiple competing interests all vying for our time. You want the head beagle to see that you are providing the type of value that can be an asset to him. And the more successful the head beagle, the more demands are made to get a small snippet of his time. The spin crafted to tell your story has to be compelling, authentic, and polished enough to capture the attention of *the head beagle*, in a nanosecond.

Everyone has expertise that is a unique combination of one's own experience, skills, education, credentials, and background in life. This unique combination must demonstrate that you are indeed a master in your field. It does not matter if you are an entrepreneur, a hair stylist, a business management consultant, or a comedian; you need to position yourself as a master. It is not enough to be good at what you do. You need to be perceived as being better than everyone else at what you do.

There are many articles about personal branding that emphasize defining your core brand attributes—all true, but also unintentionally misleading. More than anything, you need to show how your brand is not different for the sake of being different, but is superior to other brands. Want to be thought of as a master? No disrespect intended, but you actually have to behave as if you are at the top of your game and do the hard work, day after day, that it takes to become exceptional. You also need to take the time to be well versed in everything that is going on in your field. You can't just go into LinkedIn and nab someone's summer reading list and make it your own. You have to read vast numbers of books and articulate strong key concepts in your own words. You have to know who's who in your industry and sector. To be a master, you must do your own thinking!

Thoroughly research your area of expertise. Be more than a walking Wikipedia to the business issues and marketing trends that impact your business. Remember, real libraries still do exist. Use them. When was the last time you checked out an academic or white paper in your field? Go beyond using Google for research, but do use Google & Giga alerts, Twilerts and RSS feeds as filters to stay current on all the news impacting your business.

P.R. is ultimately about establishing influence. Define your key influencers, *your head beagles*. Who can make or break you? Do more than make a list of the who's who in your industry, the usual top performers, experts, and key media who cover issues relevant to your industry. Make a list of people who are so famous in the field that they really do not have the time to get to know you. Then find a way to be introduced to them. (A good P.R. person will make the connection for you.) Before reaching out to key influencers, analyze what you can do for them. Be prepared to bring significant value to the relationship.

How will you stay in touch with your key influencers? You have many ways to communicate to key influencers: by email, social media, mobile, traditional letters, or face-to-face meetings.

One way to stay in touch with your influencers is by creating superb multimedia or written content. Depending on your field or expertise, some people, especially entertainers, are best suited to video, and others—business leaders, entrepreneurs, and authors—must write reams of content that demonstrate their intelligence as innovators and thought leaders. Create articles that are informative, present a new perspective, and shed insight on developments that are relevant to your business. Publish your original articles on business networking sites and media outlets that want your innovative content. If what you've written is not innovative, clever, or truly original, then scrap it. You're better off to spend the time making the acquaintance of a new head beagle than you are to put out an article that demonstrates mediocrity instead of your strengths.

If you feel you must be perceived as a master and you cannot write well, then hire a good writer. Don't create the same old tired content that has already been done *ad nauseam*. Do not demonstrate your master prowess by using the same overused quotes of famous people like Albert Einstein, Mahatma Gandhi, or Steve Jobs. Want to be thought of as a master? Then you should be clever enough to come with an original quote or two. If you can't afford to hire writers and still want to be perceived as a thought leader, then choose another P.R. tool to tell your story in multimedia or video. If you cannot find affinity for the right P.R. vehicle, then maybe you should rethink your calling in life. Some people are meant to be spear-carriers, not leaders, and maybe you belong working in the customer service department of Home Depot. No shame to that; at least you'll get health insurance benefits when all the entrepreneurs are scrambling to pay their own.

You need to be brutally honest about your strengths and weaknesses to assess the best P.R. tools for you to use. Some people will never have the right look to be in video or the talent to write original and compelling blogs and articles. It is damaging to pursue a medium that will make you look awful. You can't demonstrate that you are a master by being perceived as less than exceptional.

To Blog or Not to Blog?

I am very cautious about advising clients to blog, because you need to consistently turn out good content. If you are not a writer, then do not start a blog. According to Technorati, 90 percent of all blogs are abandoned by their owners. Be honest with yourself. If you lack the writing talent, discipline, or "big ideas," then don't blog. Instead be an occasional guest blogger on a site that reaches your industry.

Leverage Social Media But Don't Take It Too Seriously

Post your articles, posts, and media placement to social media. The most surefire way of enlarging the audience for your writing or multimedia is to post the links to social media, especially to the royal three: Facebook, LinkedIn, and Twitter. For example, use Twitter as a tool for business intelligence or competitive intelligence to see who is out there and shares your competitive landscape and what they might be doing. But validate everything. Build your following to be a community-of-interest, composed of real people who want to hear what you have to say.

There are many other social and business sites specific to your field. Find them and use them wisely. Keep in mind, there is an enormous glut of social media, so much so that soon social media will be increasingly dismissed and minimized as a way to assess your reputation. Word-of-mouth has always been the best referral source of all. In the next few years, word-of-mouth is going to be more important than ever. People will be picking up the phone to create buzz, to get information about you, and to give the real scoop on you—all without leaving messy digital footprints. One more reason to secure powerful strategic alliances with key head beagles

Develop "You" as a Brand. Before you sign on to any social media site or reach out to any key influencer or journalist, you need to first decide exactly what you will do when you get there. If you are not clear and focused, you will waste your time, which can seriously damage your overall strategy. You're never just developing a P.R. campaign; you're developing a brand. And to build your brand, you will develop many P.R. campaigns. Use social media, but spend no more than 15 minutes a day on social media. Now everyone must create a professional brand that is constantly expanding. Your mission is powerful and unstoppable—your mission is to grow new followers. You must constantly enlarge your audience. Your followers, your friends, your clients, your audience, are people who get value from what you have to say. You must find them, identify them and get them to be part of your community. While technology forces us to move at a rapid pace, the process of growing a business still takes time and is about building a *slow-cooked brand*.

How Do You Get to the Next Level?

You may want to get greater recognition for your work and your reputation. You may want to go to the next level, but how do you get there? The answer is P.R. You have to meet the right people who are willing to be champions of your cause. These *head beagles* are your allies and advocates. These people are powerful in their own right and will influence how the public and the press will perceive you. You also have to generate your own press because it is the single most powerful tool that gives credibility to your work and your reputation. And before you generate press, you need to create a strategy that will resonate with the people whom you need to gain as your allies. Never Stop Networking. The overarching umbrella of networking includes speaking opportunities, events, and partnerships. But it also includes identifying key influencers in your field who can help your business grow and who can refer business to you. No matter what new technology or tool comes into play, it is still about people meeting people.

Get Speaking Engagements

Speak to key influencers, *head beagles*, in your industry. Only choose the best or most prestigious conferences and grand events. Unless you need to practice and hone your presentation skills, don't waste your time with organizations that will not pay you a speaking fee. Exception to this rule: When you want to meet the people face-to-face who are attending the event. If you are not good enough to command a speaking fee, then you are better off utilizing the *recluse shtick* like a *Thomas Pynchon*. Chances are he's terrible at public speaking, which is why he fancies himself as a recluse and does not make public appearances.

Put In the Time You Need to Actually Become a Master in Your Field
Becoming a master is not an overnight process. In fact, it is a lifelong pursuit. You must commit yourself to a definite period of time, at least five years, to build the initial foundation for your reputation as a master. It takes discipline, persistence, and the right type of outreach to the key influencers in your profession. Either you are destined to be a master or expert or thought leader, i.e., someone who really thinks about things, or you are not. Here is the test: Are you genuinely excited when you see a connection in history, science, art, or literature to new trends that are emerging in your field? If your answer is yes, then being a master in your field might be right for you.

Joe Boldan, entrepreneur, co-founder, and CEO for 16 years of the adventure travel apparel company *ExOfficio*, told me that most entrepreneurs fail not so much because they run out of money, but because they run out of stamina. For the past nine years, Joe has been a faculty member at the University of Washington, teaching about "Workplace Politics." He is also a workplace politics strategist and executive coach. Using P.R. tools to build awareness for your brand takes the same level of focus, stamina, and entrepreneurial acumen that it takes to build a business. The effort must be sustained for years. There are no shortcuts. Building a brand or building a business is true to the old adage: the woman who wakes up one morning and finds herself suddenly famous has not been asleep for ten years. You must spend time every day both planning and waging your own P.R. campaign. Another term for P.R. is *strategic business development*. All good P.R. drives business. And don't ever forget that.

12

The Exceptional Entrepreneur

When I was growing up in Yonkers, New York, I didn't know I was among the *working class*. My parents seemed humbled by their own life circumstances and yet they exuded a sort of class pride, a form of stalwart grace that accompanies the ordinary working people. They had this notion that they were middle class, quite righteous and carrying the whole world on their backs. I inherited the right to carry the world on my back and it's part of who I am. My mettle has been tested numerous times. It is an awesome power to know that no matter what, I can survive, flourish, and come up with a new way of doing things. Strength, true grit, determination, and discipline, all of these things make me an entrepreneur. And anyone who is committed to waging his or her own P.R. campaign must inevitably think like an entrepreneur.

As much as entrepreneurs are the saving grace and true engine of economic growth in America, based on a per-capita numbers, there has been a decline in the number of entrepreneurs. A recent story featured in *Washington Monthly*[48] states that since the 1970s, the number of entrepreneurs created in the US has been in decline.

The reasons for the decline in entrepreneurship in America are manifold: increased taxes and regulations, onerous healthcare requirements, and lack of funding. At the heart of this issue, you will find economic inequality leads to economic discrimination, which creates a culture of *opportunity inequality*. The poor, working class, and middle class have less access to high quality education, fewer job opportunities, and most important of all, it is more challenging than ever for people who are not rich to start up and build new businesses.

Entrepreneurs play a critical role in the creation of new jobs, but research indicates that fewer new businesses are being created. The numbers are down for small businesses and startups. For example, a recent article, "Why America Is Losing Its Entrepreneurial Edge,"[49] cites economists Ian Hathaway of Ennsyte Economics and Robert Litan of the Brookings Institution who documented four decades of "Declining Business Dynamism in the United States." Apparently, Hathaway and Litan examined the numbers from all fifty states and many metropolitan areas to conclude that the numbers of small businesses are on the decrease, and at the same time, the numbers have increased for companies that are "going out of business."

Many entrepreneurs—who don't come from wealth and don't have access to trust funds—bootstrap their businesses, or rely on a pool of friends and family, or angel investors to get funding. The traditional ways to get funding have contracted since the collapse of the housing market and financial markets in 2008. After all, back in 2000, many entrepreneurs could use the equity in their homes to fund a new business or to expand an existing business.

There have been some other indicators that the reason for the decline in the number of small businesses might also be due to other factors. In a recent article written by Phyllis Korkki, assignment editor of the Business section of *The New York Times*, she indicated that the fewer number of startups among the Millennial generation could be due to an enormous burden of student loans coupled with unstable employment opportunities.[50]

The economy may take many years to recover from the economic meltdown of 2008. It is also important to mention that the job market as we have known it in the past will never be the same type of job market again. With the increasing adoption of robotics and artificial intelligence, the job market is undergoing a major paradigm shift more radical than the last decade. In the late 1990s until present time, there was an increasing tendency for large companies, especially in manufacturing and technology, to outsource work to offshore teams in India, China, and Vietnam. With the emerging technology of robotics, even offshore deployment will no longer be needed. Stable employment can be a boon to starting up a business. And yet with the latest economic indicators showing a decrease in the unemployment rate, there is sufficient evidence that new job creation continues to be stalled and the labor market is still lacking roughly 10.9 million jobs.[51]

Not only are fewer jobs being created, but with the latest changes in technology, robotics, and artificial intelligence, many old jobs are being destroyed. According to recent research by the Brookings Institution,[52] for the past few decades, there has been a steady decline of new businesses and the reasons are manifold. Fewer businesses and jobs means the competition for jobs, minds, and hearts is more fierce than ever. The competition for job opportunities and resources is likely to grow even more competitive. In America, new job creation will continue to shrink at a faster rate. So if you think jobs are tight now, the job market will grow even tighter.

Ironic as it might seem, many entrepreneurs may not be able to start a new business unless they have a job. One would think that, practically speaking, having a job would interfere with starting a new business, when the reality dictates the only way to get the funds to start a business may be derived from working in a formal job to support dual goals. For many small businesses and individuals, the credit markets are still frozen. Many small businesses are being bootstrapped with dwindling savings and 401ks. In downtimes, people are more willing to fight for market share. We will, undoubtedly, see an uptick of competition for a slice of a pie that has also grown smaller.

The Exceptional Entrepreneur

Ralph Waldo Emerson is the champion of the entrepreneur, and if you closely examine his essay *Self-Reliance*, you will see it is indeed an anti-corporate manifesto. "Society everywhere is in conspiracy against the manhood of its members. Society is a joint-stock company, in which the members agree for the better securing of his bread to each shareholder, to surrender the liberty and culture of the eater. The virtue in most requests is conformity. Self-reliance is its aversion. It loves not realities and creators, but names and customs." Entrepreneurs need to become exceptional business people so their goods, products, or services can be found in the midst of all the clutter. If you think like an entrepreneur, regardless of whether you have a job, you are constantly on the hunt for opportunities; you make opportunities, and you seize opportunities. You know how to create something out of nothing.

Ralph Waldo Emerson wrote in *Self-Reliance*, "A sturdy lad from New Hampshire or Vermont, who in turn, tries all the professions, who teams it, farms it, peddles, keeps a school, preaches, edits a newspaper, goes to congress, buys a township, and so forth, in successive years, and always like a cat falls on his feet, is worth a hundred of these city dolls."

In today's terms, Emerson's definition of city dolls would undoubtedly mean the young who are indeed rich and whose first jobs coming out of college are working in the family business or as a summer intern for the family foundation. These young people could fall into the trap of viewing themselves as consistently hitting triples when they were born on third base. The downside of such a belief system is the lack of strength, wisdom, and entrepreneurial toughness that comes from failing on one's own merits.

What makes business exciting is the continual process of birth, failure, innovation, discovery, expansion, and contraction. Without analyzing the many reasons for the slowdown in new business creation, one operating premise can be asserted: individuals, from all industries and sectors, must understand how to build strong brands. Whether you are an individual or the spokesperson for a business or organization, the same rule applies—using P.R. to build your brand and manage your reputation is no longer a luxury, but is a matter of survival. The most important asset of any business or enterprise is its people, and especially people who have a clearly defined sense of their own worth. Knowing your brand is embracing what you are worth and not from solely a financial perspective. Knowing what you are worth means being aware of how to communicate

the value of the creativity, intelligence, and unique experience that you are bringing to the table in any endeavor.

Everyone is an Entrepreneur

The essence of good spin that sustains over the course of time is ultimately grounded in truth and in your hard work. Your spin will be defined in the belief you have in yourself, in your own reputation, and in your own business. The people who succeed in life are the ones who assume from the start that if they don't work hard they could fail. This is especially true for entrepreneurs, who need tremendous courage to begin their own business ventures. That courage is what must carry you during the times when the going gets tough. While you are growing a brand and managing your reputation, there will inevitably be bumps in the road, false starts and catastrophic situations that will challenge your ability to persevere. The longer you stay the course and keep learning, persisting in trying different scenarios and methods, the greater the likelihood that you will get what you want from business and from life.

Mogul Entrepreneurs: The Appetite of Genghis Khan

Some entrepreneurs who came from modest beginnings had the vision and drive to build an empire with the same force and determination as Genghis Khan. Nearly 800 years after his death, scientists from the Russian Academy of Sciences believe Genghis Khan spawned the 16 million male descendants who carry his DNA, which means during his lifetime he must have fathered thousands of children.

If Genghis Khan had interviewed for a job and was asked *What is your greatest strength?*, he would have said: *I want to conquer the world and take no prisoners*. This is the primary reason why mogul entrepreneurs steer away from job interviews and build their own business empires.

The 21st century mogul entrepreneurs Jeff Bezos of Amazon, Larry Ellison of Oracle, and Steve Jobs of Apple share three characteristics in common with one another that are also core traits of Genghis Khan. First, as children they were abandoned by one or both parents. Second, they are never satisfied with the status quo. Third, they are driven by a great egoic need to remake the world according to their own vision.

Jeff Bezos' mother was a teenager at the time of his birth, and her short-lived marriage left her as a single parent. She later remarried, but Jeff Bezos grew up without knowing his natural father. Described in an article on Portfolio.com, Jeff Bezos "is at once a happy-go-lucky mogul and a notorious micromanager: an executive who wants to know about everything from contract minutiae to how he is quoted in all Amazon press releases." Sounding very much like he is a fan of Ralph Waldo Emerson's great essay *Self-Reliance*, Jeff Bezos himself describes his business acumen as, "Invention requires a long-term willingness to be misunderstood." [Ralph Waldo Emerson said "To be great is to be misunderstood."]

Larry Ellison, born in New York City to an unwed mother, was nine months old when he contracted pneumonia, and his teenage birth mother was unable to care for him. She arranged to have him adopted by her aunt and uncle who lived in Chicago. Larry Ellison did not meet his birth mother until he was 48 years old and already a success in the business world. In Ellison's own words about the drive for success, "Great achievers are driven, not so much by the pursuit of success, but by the fear of failure."

Given up for adoption by both of his birth parents, Steve Jobs said, referring to his biological parents, "They were my sperm and egg bank. That's not harsh, it's just the way it was, a sperm bank thing, nothing more." *Fortune Magazine* wrote that Steve Jobs [was] "considered one of Silicon Valley's leading egomaniacs." And in Jobs' own words, "I want to put a ding in the universe."

As for the mighty Genghis Khan, when he was a young boy and called Temüjin, his father was murdered. He tried to claim his father's place in his tribe, but they would not be led by a boy. Abandoning the boy, his mother, and his siblings, the tribe left them all to die. The following quote is attributed to the great Genghis Khan: "The greatest joy a man can know is to conquer his enemies and drive them before him. To ride their horses and take away their possessions, to see the faces of those who were dear to them bedewed with tears, and to clasp their wives and daughters in his arms."

When they start out in life, mogul entrepreneurs aren't given the best set of circumstances in which to thrive. If anything, their first encounter with the world is harsh. They aren't rich kids with trust funds and private tutors. Many of them come from relatively inauspicious and humble beginnings. Maybe the loss of one or both parents gives them an early sense of dissatisfaction with the world and a burning desire to create a vision that reshapes reality into a world that satisfies them on their own terms. For more than three and a half decades, Larry Ellison's Oracle has been the leader in database software. Jeff Bezos and Steve Jobs have not sired 16 million descendants, but to date, over 3 million Kindles have been sold and there are over 300 million iPhone users. It could be asserted these men have conquered the world, metaphorically speaking, one electronic device at a time.

Women Entrepreneurs: Would Boudica wear Spanx?
Women entrepreneurs are wired very much like their male counterparts. However, a primary difference between them lies in the vehicles (products and services) they use to build their empires. A major angel investor in high tech companies who is a woman told me she didn't like to invest in ventures led by women because they didn't have the vision of male entrepreneurs like Jeff Bezos, Larry Ellison, or Steve Jobs. Some women build large businesses, she explained, but they're usually based on girly products. Women don't build companies that are based on disruptive technologies and have the power to change the world. Even Amazon, a name associated with ancient women warriors, took the efforts of a man to build it.

There is one woman in history who might have built a company that changed the world if she had lived in the 21st century instead of AD 60. Boudica,[53] Queen of a Celtic tribe in Britain, was married to Prasutagus, who had ruled the Iceni as an independent kingdom and ally of Rome. He willed his kingdom jointly to his daughters and the Roman Empire, but when he died, the Romans took full control. Boudica was reportedly flogged, her daughters were raped, Roman financiers called in their loans, and the kingdom was annexed as if it had been conquered in battle.

Boudica—who reportedly had long flowing hair, a loud voice, an intense glare, and wore a torc, the equivalent of a 40 pound neck ring, usually worn by male warriors of high rank—was chosen to lead her people in an assault against the Romans. Reports estimate that 80,000 were left dead and the city of Camulodunum (Colchester) was destroyed. Roman historian Tacitus said that the Britons had no desire to take prisoners— they simply slaughtered everyone in their path.

The most famous women entrepreneurs of our times are strong, powerfully intelligent women, and yet their empires are based on girly things. Diane von Furstenberg sells dresses, Estee Lauder sold makeup. Martha Stewart sells housewares. Sara Blakely built an empire on the body shaping undergarment Spanx. And Oprah Winfrey sells hope. These women didn't change the world, unless you count wearing Spanx under your suit the same as wearing game-changing armor in battle or the boardroom.

There is no indication that any of these women would ride bare breasted while they charged heroically into battle to defeat the Romans. Being Boudica in today's business world means women have the power to raise capital for girly things like dresses, makeup, duvet covers, and of course, hope. Oprah Winfrey made a career out of making women feel good about being fat and still wearing gorgeous clothes and makeup, gushing about loving themselves for just the way they are—with Spanx. Note that Spanx skyrocketed to overnight success when it was featured as one of Oprah's favorite new products.

In the next ten years as women are educated in the STEM disciplines that form the thinking for innovative technology, it will be interesting to see if more women create companies that change the world. It could be argued that Spanx, with revenues of $250 million a year, has already changed the world. So long as a premium is placed on women looking good instead of being powerful, then major investors will bet on men. The question is, would Boudica wear Spanx? The answer is: with all of her warrior activity, Boudica was probably in great shape and didn't need to wear spandex. Truth be told: in battle, Boudica wore blue body paint to look awesome, fierce, and truly powerful.

Entrepreneurial Deployment

Here is a quick summary of how the individual wages his or her own P.R. campaign with the intensity, passion, and focus of an entrepreneur. Your goal is to get greater recognition for your work and you create the right messaging to manage your reputation. You are always seeking a way to get to the next level. Like Rose Freedman, you know how to follow the rich to the top. You are actively pursuing introductions to *the head beagles* who are willing to be your allies. You are generating your own press because you know it is the single most powerful tool that gives credibility to your work and your reputation. Before you generate press, you know you need to create a strategy that will resonate with the people you need to gain as your allies. There is one other factor that is essential to becoming a successful entrepreneur and winning your P.R. campaign. You have to know when to break the law.

Break the Law

There are many ways to approach P.R. with an entrepreneurial mindset that wins hearts and minds. First, you must break the law. The rule we pretend to abide by is that Americans are law-abiding citizens, but the real rule is break the law, but don't get caught. As a child growing up in New York I realized there were two sets of rules: the written and the unwritten, the spoken and the unspoken. To put it in the Bronx vernacular: *there was the thing everyone said they did when they went to church on Sunday; then there were the things they really did.*

Recently, I was on the phone with a major venture capitalist that I will refer to as *Bernie Salkowitz* to protect his identity. Bernie was talking about who gets venture money and who does not. Then the subject meandered on to human nature. "People, being human," he said, "never do what they say they're going to do. They say one thing and do another. This is America. Americans are, after all, human. They want to break the law. It's healthy to want to break the law. When you think about it, you should break the law."

Call it another American paradox, but don't admit your predilection for wanting to break the law in a public forum. Frankly, being compelled to honestly and righteously break the law is not something we can openly discuss in our culture; it is somewhat akin to being a sin. There are people who would not understand and it is not your job to educate them. Some secrets are best kept to one's self. A desire to break the law should not be shared with, say… law enforcement officials, anyone affiliated with a political party, your teacher, your boss, your co-workers, your clients, and anyone who might be inclined to use negative information against you—this latter category includes most people.

Regarding law, there are many sets of rules that have been recorded since the beginning of time. The Code of Hammurabi speaks of harsh consequences such as whacking off whole body parts and limbs. The Justinian Code, another set of Draconian measures, set the tone for the Greco-Roman world that had their time and place, but no longer present as the source code for modernity. You don't have to go far to learn of current accounts of laws as severe as the Codes of Justinian or Hammurabi. Muslim women whose only sin is the desire to go to school are stoned to death by the Taliban. Men in the Arab world who dishonor their families by working for the wrong tribal leader are put to death in the most gruesome fashion possible in the local town square.

Then there are the secular decrees that frame the ideal for human aspirations and liberty, and provide the foundation for

Western culture: Magna Carta, The Declaration of Independence, and The US Constitution. Now that you have become more educated in *American Spin*, never be deceived by thinking laws are solely architected to protect society. Codes, laws, rules, fair or not, religious or not, share one underlying principle in common: to control the inherent unruly nature of the human being. And you can be sure that the rationale behind most laws is intended to benefit the Divine Right of Kings. The saving grace of American culture is its historical legacy built on dissidents, revolutionaries, and religious zealots who left other countries in pursuit of freedom.

The American cultural imperative is living in a state that is constantly on the verge of erupting into anarchy. Everyone is on the take and everyone has a price. As Americans, we like to create laws but we also like to break them. Finding a loophole, dodging the bullet, it is the American way. We are a cowboy culture. There are individuals who have inherited the Divine Right of Kings, who really like law because they are in control and they want to retain their power.

As much as Americans uphold the law, there is a pervading distrust of any law. At the heart of American culture, our democratic values enable us all to voice a healthy skepticism of law, social order, and the government. It is part of our enduring American legacy to question authority. Despite a penchant for authority, it is still a fundamental drive in every American to want to break the law.

An underlying American value is to evaluate every law for the sole purpose to consider breaking the law. Every day, Americans encounter laws they choose to break. The decision whether or not to break a law is usually governed by a risk analysis. We ask ourselves questions: How much trouble will I get into if I get caught? Is breaking this law worth the risk of my getting caught? My advice: break the law, but don't get caught.

Most of the time, I am a responsible adult and I do follow the law. Advising people to break the law sounds like a terrible thing to say to honest people. However, when you consider that the whole notion of law is rooted in authority that tends to control the populace to benefit the rich, it is not so strange after all. Emerson said, "Our leaders are slaves to public opinion and do not make decisions based on integrity. They are all about winning and power and not about doing the right thing." Whether or not you choose to break the law needs to be evaluated on a case-by-case basis to establish the true merits of the law and to examine why it was made. Ask yourself: who will benefit?

In *Le Père Goriot* published in *Revue de Paris* in 1834, Honoré Balzac said, "Behind every great fortune there is a crime." He did not elaborate on the type or size of crime. Crime to one person might be civil disobedience to another. I'm not encouraging you to arbitrarily break the law. I can only emphasize that it is important to break the law when the law is simply not working. You have to weigh the risks. Assess the benefit to you (as well as others) against the potential outcome. Some laws were made to keep people safe and some were not. Some laws were made for economic and political reasons and can be a form of arbitrary oppression. A brief historical rendition of oppressive American law would include: Slavery, discrimination against women, minorities and gays, the poor, the mentally ill, and unfair treatment to workers through the Industrial Age. Even in America, people have lost their liberty and have been treated unfairly in the name of the law!

The American Judicial system has designed law so it can be broken for a higher good. Breaking the law with honor is based on the principles of civil disobedience. Recall the examples made by Martin Luther King and Rosa Parks and Mahatma Gandhi, who employed non-violent actions to break the law. Always remember, people make laws. American laws are alive and fluid; and they were designed to evolve over time and be changed. Instead of breaking the law, you can take initiative and make change happen. If you have the time, motivation, and money, you can change the law by working through the system. But if you don't have the time, motivation, and money, there is an alternative. You can learn to become sneaky smart.

Are You Sneaky Smart?

If you weren't born into wealth, admittedly you cannot afford a high profile P.R. firm to build your brand and manage your reputation. To gain advantage, you need to become sneaky smart.

Sneaky smart is not scary smart. Scary smart belongs to the realm of the geeks at MIT and Stanford. When you're scary smart, sometimes you frighten people away. It's like having a microchip in your brain that makes you speak in an algorithm no one can understand.

When you're sneaky smart, no one saw exactly what you were doing to succeed. It's the genius equivalent of being *sneaky fast*. Stories abound about being sneaky fast in sports. In baseball, it usually has to do with players stealing bases. Sneaky fast is about superb athletic movement. In football, the athlete's body is so well trained and coordinated that everything works together seamlessly and no one can see just how fast the athlete is moving. Check out this story about Kentucky Wildcats quarterback Patrick Towles.[54]

When your learning is sneaky fast, you don't even realize you have mastered the material. The synapses are firing and you soaked up the content like a sponge. All of which brings us to the concept of *sneaky smart*. Successful entrepreneurs are sneaky smart. While they work hard, you don't notice how the way in which they work is very smart; they're industrious, habitual doers, and all of their activity seems effortless. The sneaky smart are always pursuing a new project, a new dream, or a new theory, and when they encounter an obstacle or a setback, they leverage it into a new opportunity. Most important of all, sneaky smart people know when to break the rules.

The sneaky smart don't accept rules on face value and follow them blindly. They will weigh the rules and ponder how they affect them (as well as others). So think through every law carefully. Consider each law in how it affects you (as well as others). Obey laws that make sense and were written to protect and advocate for the people. Recognize laws that were made to favor the Divine Right of Kings to pander to their interests.

The key is to recognize the difference and act accordingly. They obey laws that make sense, but they also know when it is time to break the law. The sneaky smart have a maverick spirit and the strong desire not to be regulated and caught up in someone else's game. The sneaky smart know if you always play by someone else's rules, you will not win. Sound unethical? Think again. There isn't anything wrong with stealing bases, not when you're competing against the superrich who behave as though they've hit a triple when they were really born on third base. Being sneaky smart means becoming a master at spotting the right moment to steal all of the bases and to drive home.

All of us encounter roadblocks. Some encounter more obstacles than others. There is a whole array of commonplace scenarios. You find yourself going into a job interview. The company knew whom they were going to hire, only you did not know. The job was already wired from inside the company. You never stood a chance. Your book just can't get published. A similar book in terms of content and genre but of lesser literary merit does get published. You never knew the right editor.

The list of potential roadblocks is endless. The movie role is never offered—to you. The recording contract is never drafted. The promotion never happens. The application to college or graduate school is rejected. Entrance to your favorite nightclub is denied. You are denied financing, a mortgage, a high limit credit card. If you think life is unfair, doling out its rewards and punishments at random, or that everything is wired against you, then you're right. You haven't networked successfully. You have not made it a priority to know the right people. You did not place yourself in a position of success by becoming a master.

You can only walk through the doors that will open to you. Sometimes you can persevere and bang your head against a door that will not budge. Sooner or later you have to cut your losses and move onto the next door that will spring open. In this incredible journey we call life, you can only find out who you are and who you are not. There are times when you may be allowed entrée into a world that under ordinary circumstances—

for one reason or another—would have been closed off to you. Luck, timing, sheer talent, hard work, and persistent devotion to networking may be riding with you. The same elements of luck, timing, sheer talent, hard work, and networking also help to explain how a black woman, Oprah Winfrey, rose to be a media icon and two white boys, Eminem and Macklemore, became rap stars. Once you are given access to a new world, you will be treated indistinguishably from those who think they had the original right to be there. More importantly, your very performance will often be perceived as more heroic than those who didn't have to struggle because they inherited the Divine Right of Kings.

Be a good steward of your own resources, especially of your time. Make money, work hard, make your own luck, be lucky, be sneaky smart, network constantly, exhaust your contacts, and use every resource made available to you, and where none are apparent, create your own resources, make something out of nothing. The author Alice Walker said, "The most common way people give up their power is by thinking they don't have any." Stick up for yourself, because if you don't, no one else will. Ironically, when you do stick up for yourself, you will be surprised at how many people will rally to offer you support. Americans adore a hero, the maverick, the lone cowboy, and the first one out in front of a movement like Gloria Steinem or a new icon in popular culture like *Madonna* or *Lady Gaga*. To be a successful entrepreneur and to wage a good P.R. campaign, you have to trust yourself. When you trust yourself, you develop self-reliance, and there is no greater gift that you could give to the world. In America if you have sheer talent, true grit, and you work hard as an entrepreneur, you can still succeed—this is the essence of *American Spin* and it's good spin because it's true.

References*

The James Bond Bedside Companion, non-fiction, encyclopedic work by Raymond Benson was first published in 1984.

Edward Bernays classic treatise on *Propaganda*, originally published in 1928.

The Big Short: Inside the Doomsday Machine is a non-fiction book by Michael Lewis about the build-up of the housing and credit bubble during the 2000s that ultimately led to the crash of 2008. The book was released on March 15, 2010, by W. W. Norton & Company.

The Shallows: What the Internet Is Doing to Our Brains is a 2010 book by American journalist Nicholas G. Carr, published by W. W. Norton & Company.

Management Challenges for the 21st Century, Peter F. Drucker, published by HarperBusiness, 2001.

American Vertigo: Traveling America in the Footsteps of Tocqueville is a 2006 book by Bernard-Henri Lévy, Translated by Charlotte Mandell, published by Random House.

Who Killed Daniel Pearl? by Bernard-Henri Lévy, is a 2006 book, translated from the French by James X, published by Mitchell Melville House.

Self-Reliance, an essay by Ralph Waldo Emerson, first published in 1841.

*Most of the articles selected as references were sourced due to their adherence to a higher standard of journalism that indicated the information was derived from investigative reporting and not solely from the spin of P.R. professionals.

Notes

[1]*The Shallows: What the Internet Is Doing to Our Brains*, by American journalist Nicholas G. Carr, W. W. Norton & Company, 2010.

[2]"Yellow journalism, or the yellow press, is a type of journalism that presents little or no legitimate well-researched news and instead uses eye-catching headlines to sell more newspapers. Techniques may include exaggerations of news events, scandal-mongering, or sensationalism. By extension, the term yellow journalism is used today as a pejorative to decry any journalism that treats news in an unprofessional or unethical fashion." From "Yellow Journalism," *Wikipedia*.
http://en.wikipedia.org/wiki/Yellow_journalism

[3]"These 6 Corporations Control 90 percent Of The Media In America," *Business Insider*, June 14, 2012.
http://www.businessinsider.com/these-6-corporations-control-90-of-the-media-in-america-2012-6

[4]"Four Times a Charm? Rupert Murdoch, Single Again, Seems to Need Dating Advice," Brooks Barnes, *The New York Times*, December 13, 2013.
http://www.nytimes.com/2013/12/15/fashion/rupert-murdoch-single-again-seems-to-need-dating-advice.html

[5]Jesus Christ did not mean a sewing needle. He was referring to a gate named Needle entering into the city of Jerusalem that was so narrow, camels could not squeeze through.

[6]Jayson Blair is the former journalist with *The New York Times* who resigned in 2003 after it was discovered that he plagiarized and fabricated his news stories. This isn't to suggest that all *New*

York Times reporters conduct their journalistic practices like Blair. It is, however, being asserted in *American Spin* that many stories are placed in *The New York Times* as well as many other publications because a well-connected spinmeister pitched the publication.

"Times Reporter Who Resigned Leaves Long Trail of Deception," *The New York Times*, May 11, 2013.
http://www.nytimes.com/2003/05/11/national/11PAPE.html

[7]"Amid Criticism, Support for Media's Watchdog Role Stands Out," *Pew Research Center*, August 8, 2013.
http://www.people-press.org/2013/08/08/amid-criticism-support-for-medias-watchdog-role-stands-out/

[8]Literary scholars have asserted that Umberto Eco borrowed "The Name of the Rose" from William Shakespeare.

[9]Places named for Benjamin Franklin
http://en.wikipedia.org/wiki/List_of_places_named_for_Benjamin_Franklin

*There are a total of 151 places and institutions listed: 1 state, 32 counties, 50 municipalities (that is, towns and cities), 3 geologic features, 6 colleges and universities, 23 high schools, 8 middle schools, 14 elementary schools (that is 51 schools in all), 2 businesses, 3 transportation ways, and 9 other things. (This list does not include retail establishments, pubs & eateries, professional services, and many other enterprises.)

[10]"Women Could have Greater Role in Church, Says Pope," *The Wall Street Journal*, May 5, 2014.
http://online.wsj.com/news/articles/SB10001424052702303369904579420532931785604;

"Pope says only men can be priests, but women must have voice in church," Catholic News Service, November 26, 2013. http://www.catholicnews.com/data/stories/cns/1304990.htm

[11]"Pope Francis for Rolling Stone," 360nobs.com, January 30, 2014. http://www.360nobs.com/2014/01/pope-francis-for-rolling-stone/

[12]"The Hillary Show," Ken Auletta, *The New Yorker*, June 2, 2014. http://www.newyorker.com/magazine/2014/06/02/the-hillary-show

[13]"Mika: What does Hillary Clinton Stand For?" *Free Beacon*, May 5, 2014. http://freebeacon.com/politics/mika-what-does-hillary-clinton-stand-for/

[14]"Teenager's Sentence in Fatal Drunken-Driving Case Stirs 'Affluenza' Debate," *The New York Times*, December 13, 2013. http://www.nytimes.com/2013/12/14/us/teenagers-sentence-in-fatal-drunken-driving-case-stirs-affluenza-debate.html

[15]"Seattle PR firm Reveals Efforts to Free Amanda Knox," *Puget Sound Business Journal*, October 21, 2011. http://www.bizjournals.com/seattle/news/2011/10/20/seattle-pr-firm-reveals-efforts-to.html

[16]"Who is Amanda Knox?" *The Guardian*, February 8, 2014. http://www.theguardian.com/world/2014/feb/08/who-is-amanda-knox-interview

[17]"Enron's Many Strands: The Ex-Chairman; Lay's Wife Defends Him and Says They're Ruined," *The New York Times*, January 29, 2001. http://www.nytimes.com/2001/01/29/business/enron-s-many-strands-ex-chairman-lay-s-wife-defends-him-says-they-re-ruined.html

[18]"Enron Wife Linda Lay Sells Off Family Treasures In PR Stunt," *Rense.com*.
http://www.rense.com/general29/stunt.htm

[19]"Accident expert says Grubman intentionally ran down people in 2001," *USA TODAY*, April 26, 2004.
http://usatoday30.usatoday.com/life/people/2004-04-26-expert-grubman_x.htm

[20]"At Lunch With: Cindy Adams; Listen Up: Lady Plugs Self, Dog, Not Stars," *The New York Times*, February 2, 2003.
http://www.nytimes.com/2003/02/02/style/at-lunch-with-cindy-adams-listen-up-lady-plugs-self-dog-not-stars.html

[21]"New York Times columnist David Pogue accused of hitting wife with iPhone," *The Hour Online*, May 19, 2011.
http://www.thehour.com/news/westport/new-york-times-columnist-david-pogue-accused-of-hitting-wife/article_c7c830d2-2db0-5f12-9b4a-cbf9a899a08a.html

[22]"Don't Publicize Your Proposal the Pogue Way," *Slate.com*, August 31, 2012.
http://www.slate.com/blogs/browbeat/2012/08/31/david_pogue_nicki_dugan_marriage_proposal_it_should_never_have_been_publicized_.html

[23]"Bank Examiner was told to back off Goldman," DealBook: A Financial News Service of *The New York Times*, October 10, 2013.
http://dealbook.nytimes.com/2013/10/10/bank-examiner-was-told-to-back-off-goldman-suit-says/

[24]"The Real Lee Radziwell," *The New York Times Style Magazine*, February 7, 2013.
http://tmagazine.blogs.nytimes.com/2013/02/07/the-real-lee-radziwill/

[25]"In Conversation: Lee Radziwill and Sofia Coppola, on Protecting Privacy," *The New York Times Style Magazine*, May 30, 2013. http://tmagazine.blogs.nytimes.com/2013/05/30/in-conversation-lee-radziwill-and-sophia-coppola-on-protecting-privacy/

[26]"On the Road Avec M. Lévy," Garrison Keillor, *The New York Times,* January 29, 2006. http://www.nytimes.com/2006/01/29/books/review/29keillor.html

[27]"Murder in Karachi," *The New York Review of Books*, December 4, 2003. http://www.nybooks.com/articles/archives/2003/dec/04/murder-in-karachi/

[28]"Dominique Strauss-Kahn Defended Witlessly By Bernard-Henri Levy And Ben Stein," *Huffington Post*, May 18, 2011. http://www.huffingtonpost.com/2011/05/18/dominique-strauss-kahn-bernard-henri-levy-ben-stein_n_863633.html

[29]"The Woody Allen Allegations: Not So Fast," *The Daily Beast*, January 27, 2014. http://www.thedailybeast.com/articles/2014/01/27/the-woody-allen-allegations-not-so-fast.html

[30]"PR Career Outlook," PR Council. http://prfirms.org/careers/pr-career-outlook

"Management Occupations," *Occupation Outlook Handbook*, The Bureau of Labor Statistics. http://www.bls.gov/ooh/management/

"Special Report on Council of Public Relations Firms," DeeperWeb Research. http://deeperweb.com/business-research/public-relations/council-of-public-relations-firms-research-trends-surveys.html

[31]"For Two Economists, the Buffett Rule Is Just a Start," *The New York Times*, April 16, 2012.
http://www.nytimes.com/2012/04/17/business/for-economists-saez-and-piketty-the-buffett-rule-is-just-a-start.html

[32]"Current State of Investigative Reporting," talk by Seymour Hersh at Boston University, May 19, 2009.
http://www.youtube.com/watch?v=yRWYa7XHMO0

[33]"Understanding the rise of sponsored content," *AmericanPress Institute*, November 13, 2013.
http://www.americanpressinstitute.org/publications/reports/white-papers/understanding-rise-sponsored-content/

[34]"Our Invisible Rich," Paul Krugman, *The New York Times*, September 28, 2014.
http://www.nytimes.com/2014/09/29/opinion/paul-krugman-our-invisible-rich.html

[35]"At Bank of America, a $4 Billion Wet Blanket on the Party, *The New York Times*, May 3, 2014.
http://www.nytimes.com/2014/05/04/business/at-bank-of-america-a-4-billion-wet-blanket-on-the-party.html

[36]"How Jamie Dimon hid the $6 billion loss," *Fortune*, July 13, 2012.
http://finance.fortune.cnn.com/2012/07/13/jpmorgan-hid-london-whale/

[37]"$2B settlement ends trade center litigation," *USA TODAY*, May 23, 2007.
http://usatoday30.usatoday.com/money/industries/insurance/2007-05-23-tradecenterinsure_N.htm

[38]"For Richer" by Paul Krugman, *The New York Times Magazine*, October 20, 2002.
http://www.nytimes.com/2002/10/20/magazine/for-richer.html

[39]"Class Conflict," *Wikipedia*.
http://en.wikipedia.org/wiki/Class_conflict

[40]" Number of People Living in 'Poverty Areas' Up, Census Bureau Reports," *United States Census Bureau Press Releases*, June 30, 2014.
http://www.census.gov/newsroom/press-releases/2014/cb14-123.html

[41]"Enron's Many Strands: Warning Signs; Credit Agencies Waited Months To Voice Doubt About Enron," *The New York Times*, February 8, 2002.
http://www.nytimes.com/2002/02/08/business/enron-s-many-strands-warning-signs-credit-agencies-waited-months-voice-doubt.html

[42]"The World's Billionaires," *Forbes*, real time listing.
http://www.forbes.com/billionaires/list;

"Stop Coddling the Super-Rich," Warren Buffett, *The New York Times*, August 14, 2011.
http://www.nytimes.com/2011/08/15/opinion/stop-coddling-the-super-rich.html

[43]"For Two Economists, the Buffett Rule Is Just a Start," Annie Lowrey, *The New York Times*, April 16, 2012.
http://www.nytimes.com/2012/04/17/business/for-economists-saez-and-piketty-the-buffett-rule-is-just-a-start.html

[44]"The Glass-Steagall Act Explained," *NerdWallet*.
http://www.nerdwallet.com/blog/banking/glass-steagall-act-explained/

[45]"Weddings: Vows; David Sloan and Judith Place," *The New York Times*, February 3, 2002.
http://www.nytimes.com/2002/02/03/style/weddings-vows-david-sloan-and-judith-place.html

[46]"Why Grubman Was So Keen To Get His Twins Into the Y: Rich and Famous New Yorkers See Preschool as a Passport to Success," *The Wall Street Journal*, November 15, 2002.
http://online.wsj.com/articles/SB10373112521116524828

[47]"James Joyce," *The New York Times Reference*.
http://topics.nytimes.com/top/reference/timestopics/people/j/james_joyce/index.html

[48]"The Slow-Motion Collapse of American Entrepreneurship: The experts tell us new business start-ups will save the American economy. So how come there are fewer and fewer of them?" Barry C. Lynn and Lina Khan, *Washington Monthly*, July/August 2012.
http://www.washingtonmonthly.com/magazine/julyaugust_2012/features/the_slowmotion_collapse_of_ame038414.php

[49]"Why America Is Losing Its Entrepreneurial Edge," *Harvard Business Review*, May 20, 2014.
http://blogs.hbr.org/2014/05/why-america-is-losing-its-entrepreneurial-edge/

[50]"The Ripple Effect of Rising Student Debt," *The New York Times*, May 24, 2014.
http://www.nytimes.com/2014/05/25/business/the-ripple-effects-of-rising-student-debt.html

[51]"Shrinking Labor Force Explains Drop in Unemployment," *Economic Policy Institute*, December 9, 2011.
http://www.epi.org/news/shrinking-labor-force-explains-drop-unemployment/

[52]"Declining Business Dynamism in the United States: A Look at States and Metros," *The Brookings Institution*, May 5, 2014. http://www.brookings.edu/research/papers/2014/05/declining-business-dynamism-litan

[53]There are many spelling variations. She is also known as Boudicca and Boadicea.

[54]"UK coach Stoops: 'Sneaky fast' Patrick Towles will usually run less," *Lexington Herald-Leader Kentucky.com*, September 7, 2014. http://www.kentucky.com/2014/09/07/3417245/stoops-sneaky-fast-patrick-towles.html

Index

A

C

Caesar Augustus 5–6
Caesar, Julius 5–6
Carr, Nicholas, Author 16
Catholic Church 3, 4, 20, 101, 116
Cavuto, Neal, American television anchor on the Fox Business Network 55
Challenger space shuttle 102–103
Class warfare 127
Clinton, Bill 54, 97, 101, 102
Clinton, Hillary Rodham 53–57
Colbert, Stephen. *See* Stewart, Jon and Stephen Colbert
College of Propaganda at Rome, Sacred College of *Propaganda Fide* 3
Content Bubble 16–20
Coppola, Sofia 105–106
Cronkite, Walter 21–23

D

Dahl, Dave, Dave's Killer Bread 39–40, 67
Dimon, James "Jamie", CEO, JPMorgan & Co 124
Divine Right of Kings 123, 125, 135, 137, 141, 174, 176, 178
Dodd-Frank Act 56
Dostoevsky, Fyodor 44–45, 45–46
Dreyfus Affair, Lieutenant Alfred Dreyfus 20, 75
Drucker, Peter F. 62, 124

E

Einstein, Albert 160
Ellison, Larry, founder, CEO, Oracle 168–170
Emerson, Ralph Waldo 25, 26, 166–167, 169, 175
Eminem 152, 178
Enron Corp. 78–82, 130, 133–134

F

Facebook 8, 10, 16, 17, 22, 34, 65, 90–91, 109, 112, 135–137, 161
Farrow, Dylan 109
FindLaw.com 10
Fitch Ratings 130, 134
Fleming, Ian 49–51
Franklin, Benjamin 47–49
Freedman, Rose 119–122, 153, 172

G

H

I

J

K

R

Radziwill, Lee 105–106
Rand, Ayn 116
Robles, Anthony, wrestler 40–42
Rushdie, Salman, author 149

S

Saez, Emmanuel and Thomas Piketty, Economists and authors 111, 127
Schadenfreude, Open Schadenfreude 83
Scheherazade 63–64
Segarra, Carmen M., Former NY Fed Examiner 102
Self-Reliance (the essay by Ralph Waldo Emerson) 26, 31, 36, 51, 104,
        147, 166–167, 169
Silverstein, Larry, World Trade Center 125
Simpson, O.J. 77
Sin 89–104, 127
Skakel, Michael 73–74
Soros, George, the chairman of Soros Fund Management 132
Spinmeister 25–26, 76–77, 81, 95, 105, 113
Spitzer, Eliot 97–98
Standard & Poor's 130, 134
Steinem, Gloria 55, 178
Stewart, Jon and Stephen Colbert 23, 104
Stewart, Rod 65–66
Strauss-Kahn, Dominique 108

T

The Titanic 59
Triangle Shirtwaist Fire 119–121
Twitter 4, 8–9, 14, 16, 18, 20, 21, 98–100, 109, 112, 136, 161
Tyco International 130, 133, 134

U

US Census Bureau 128

V

Virgin Mary 33
Vuitton, Louis 10

W

Walker, Alice, Author 178
Walking Dead 68
Wall Street Journal 21, 22, 89, 108
Warren, Elizabeth, US Senator from Massachusetts 56
Weill, Sanford "Sandy," former chief executive and chairman of Citigroup
144–145
Weiner, Anthony 99
Weinstein, Harvey, Film Producer 109
Whistleblower 102–104
Woods, Tiger 83
WorldCom 78
Wyatt, Edward, *New York Times* Reporter 130

Y

Yellow Journalism 17

Z

Zola, Émile 20, 75, 107